It's been a long time since I've read a [...] edly affirming in such a truth-telling [...] Jess has a way of gently and boldly r[...]ing all our excuses for a minute, and allowing us to freely see *who* God made us to be—the women we *already are*. What makes this message so powerful is that Jess does this in a way that is deeply rooted in Scripture, real life experiences, and genuine, authentic love for every girl who longs to be seen and understood. For any woman who's ever felt a little like she didn't belong, a little like she may not measure up, and a little like she's too messy, imperfect, or extra, this book will be a blessing to your heart, just as it was to mine.

Emily Ley, founder of Simplified and
bestselling author of *A Simplified Life*

In *You Are the Girl for the Job*, Jess Connolly pulls up a chair in front of the reader, grabs her by both shoulders, and stares her straight in the eye to tell her, in no uncertain terms, the unique value she has to herself and the world. This message is so needed and resonated deeply with me because, no matter how successful you might be, the trap of comparison can make you believe you're not quite the right person to do what you do. This book slaps away any doubt and replaces it with the truth of God's Word, combined with the loving assurance of a friend who wants you to see what she sees; a girl God picked for the task in front of her. Thank you for writing this gift for the world.

Nona Jones, Nona Jones Ministries, head of
Faith-Based Partnerships, Facebook

Have you found yourself saying, *I'm not cut out for this*, *This is too hard*, and *I'm not enough*? Me too. But books like Jess Connolly's lift our eyes and hearts to remind us that we ARE the girls for the job! Juggling and compartmentalizing and balancing can feel overwhelming, so Jess has written a manifesto for women who dare to believe we are capable of more and willing to jump into the work of calling. Jess wrote with such power and conviction not only because she believes this, but because she is living it out!

Bianca Juarez Olthoff, speaker, teacher, and
bestselling author of *Play with Fire* and
How To Have Your Life Not Suck

When we are tempted to weigh and measure our own capacity, Jess Connolly comes alongside like a friend who cheers you on, reminding you that Jesus is the hero of the story. That's the good news found in *You Are the Girl for the Job.*

Ruth Chou Simons, bestselling author of
GraceLaced and *Beholding and Becoming:
The Art of Everyday Worship*

Jess does it again. She gets in your business and messes you up. For anyone (like me) who has walked in doubt and defeat, and taken up residence there, this book will jumpstart your heart. God always fulfills what he started; we need only say yes.

Rebekah Lyons, author, *Rhythms of
Renewal* and *You Are Free*

In *You Are the Girl for the Job*, Jess writes with characteristic passion as she calls women everywhere to step into their God-given purpose. Using biblical insights, personal stories, and practical wisdom, Jess encourages and equips any woman who has ever held herself back to rise up and run towards the call of God on her life.

Jo Saxton, speaker and author of *The Dream of You*

You Are the Girl for the Job is an incredible book for women who want to use their passions, dreams, and stories to change the world. It's deeply rooted in truth, graced with stories you can relate to, and it will give you the language you need to continually encourage those around you.

Jessica Honegger, founder of Noonday Collection
and bestselling author of *Imperfect Courage*

In a season where women are awakening like never before, Jess uses *You Are the Girl for the Job* to remind us that it really is okay to roar. Heaven wants us to be seen, to be heard, and to color outside the lines. We don't have to be timid to be prove our humility or ladylikeness. We don't have to do what we've always done the way we we've always done it. And we don't even have to fully understand where we're going or how we're going to get there, as long as we dare to believe that God has indeed called us. Jess isn't just inviting us to go out and change the world. She is daring us to change our inner world in a radically disruptive, beautiful and rebellious way. By believing in our own worthiness, we give other women overdue permission to do the same!

Marshawn Evans Daniels, Godfidence Coach®,
TV personality, reinvention strategist for
women, and founder of SheProfits.com

To fully live into the life right in front of us is one of the most challenging callings we are given. Jess Connolly lovingly and wisely invites us down this path which she has not only written about in theory but has actually lived out so beautifully.

Katherine Wolf, author of *Hope Heals*

YOU ARE THE GIRL FOR THE JOB

YOU ARE THE GIRL FOR THE JOB

DARING TO BELIEVE THE
GOD WHO CALLS YOU

Jess Connolly

 ZONDERVAN®

ZONDERVAN

You Are the Girl for the Job
Copyright © 2019 by Jessica Ashleigh Connolly

Requests for information should be addressed to:
Zondervan, *3900 Sparks Dr. SE, Grand Rapids, Michigan 49546*

ISBN 978-0-310-35245-7 (softcover)

ISBN 978-0-310-35249-5 (audio)

ISBN 978-0-310-35247-1 (ebook)

Published in association with literary agent Jenni Burke of D.C. Jacobson & Associates LLC, an Author Management Company www.dcjacobson.com

Cover photography: John Hillin Photography
Cover design: Hannah Warren
Interior design: Kait Lamphere

Printed in the United States of America

19 20 21 22 23 24 25 26 /LSC/ 15 14 13 12 11 10 9 8 7 6 5 4 3 2 1

*For Ruby, who reminds me that
the hype about God is always true.*

Yet I knew the moment I started worrying about whether or not I was good enough for the job, I wouldn't be able to do it.

—MADELEINE L'ENGLE

SIX STEPS TOWARDS ABUNDANT OBEDIENCE

V. CATCH THE VISION

VI. MAKE YOUR MOVE

FOREWORD BY ANNIE F. DOWNS

I don't know I need a reminder until I do.

Do you know what I mean?

My phone alarm just went off reminding me of a lunch meeting I have today. My assistant just sent me a message that I need to return a phone call this afternoon. My sister just texted me to make sure I had a date on my calendar to go to an Atlanta United soccer game with her next month.

I love all these reminders. I need to be reminded.

The actual purpose of a reminder is to RE MIND us. To put back in our mind something we have forgotten, or maybe even never known.

Re-mind: 1. cause (someone) to remember someone or something. 2. cause someone to think of (something) because of a resemblance or likeness. 3. bring something, especially a commitment or necessary course of action, to the attention of (someone).

Jess helps me remember things. She and I sat at a dinner in 2013 until the entire restaurant was closed, all the chairs turned over on tables, all the floor swept, all the employees annoyed and ready to go home. It's a place in Germantown neighborhood in Nashville and it was warm outside. That's about all I remember except the way Jess told her story.

She looked me in the eyes the whole time. She teared up, so did I. She laughed, so did I. She laid out pieces of her heart and story that I did not know but were important for me to understand and for her to be understood. She needed to walk backwards a bit for us to walk forward. She was telling me things I didn't know, but it also felt like she was reminding me of something greater that I had always known.

I had always known I could do the thing that was right in front of me, but she reminded me that I had everything I needed.

I had always known that while the road would be tough and it wouldn't always be easy- the going backwards into my own story and going forward into my calling- but she reminded me how much it mattered, because she did it too.

I had always wanted a cheerleader to tell me I was the girl for the job, and Jess reminded me.

Jess also causes me to think of some people I really love because of the resemblance or likeness. She reminds me of my mom, a strong business woman who knows her professional strength. She reminds me of my friend Haley, a stay at home mom who finds joy and purpose and strength in raising her children. She reminds me of my pastor Kevin who teaches us to pray, who turns to God first, and loves the local church so deeply. She reminds me of my friend Nicolle who works out regularly because her entire self is better because she cares about her health. And she reminds me of Jesus because of her resemblance to Him. She models strength and balance and joy and all these things I see in my relationship with Him.

Jess has done all that for me. But now I get to remind you. I get to focus on that third definition of "remind". I want to bring something to your attention. It is a necessary course of action.

You are the girl for the job.

Jess is the girl to remind you.

To God be the glory.

MY SPIN CLASS REVELATION

I sat on a bike in a dark and emo cycling studio. The room was shadowy, with lights that rose and fell, evoking emotion, matching the rise and fall of our intensity. The music was loud—so loud the words were almost indistinguishable, but the impact wasn't diminished. There was a thumping, a thriving undertone set by the sound, and it was perceived by everyone in the room. I'd come in that morning defeated, to say the least, jet-lagged and heartsick from an incredibly hard season, but I found myself swept up in the passion and energy in the absolute best way.

It was a 7 a.m. spin class in Los Angeles. I was on the West Coast for a work trip, and the whole week, I'd honestly felt like a character in a romantic comedy. You know, the one where the woman gets scorned by her lover and rushes off to see some new piece of the world, only to find herself and figure out that she was all she really needed in the first place? Okay—that wasn't *quite* the story I was living, but I was a broken gal, temporarily in a new place, praying for a fresh wind and hoping for some healing.

I'd come to LA fresh on the heels of an incredibly painful season in our church. I'm a pastor's wife—a church planter's wife, to be exact—and while some moments of leading the church are exhilarating and we feel like we're seeing in new colors, other seasons are heartbreaking, and it feels like signing up to run on mission is the same as signing up to have your heart poked by toothpicks incessantly for years. We'd recently sat through meeting after meeting after meeting, handling our own shortcomings and sorting through the pain of the people we love the most—pain we'd caused, pain they'd caused, all of it hard and all of it broken.

This work trip had been planned in the midst of it, so while leaving felt like the absolute last thing that I wanted to do, it was what I had to do, and I was trying to make the most of it. I packed my sunglasses and my most West Coast-y clothes (lots of black!) and hopped on the plane, eager to see what God had for me on the other side. As I made the almost-all-day trek from Charleston, SC, to LAX, I found a sliver of airplane internet and booked a bike at my favorite spin place, Soul Cycle, for a 7 a.m. class.

Have you ever been to Soul Cycle? It's a mix between a dance club, a fitness class, and a really incredible worship service. I basically can't get enough of it. Right now you can only find a true Soul Cycle class in pretty large cities, so anytime I'm in a bigger city, I figure out how to make my way toward one. Austin; LA; Washington, DC; New York—if I'm in one of those spots, I'm heading to Soul Cycle.

So far, I haven't made it through a class without crying—not because the physicality of the exercise is so tough, but because the experience is so moving for me. It's the perfect combination for my personality to feel alive. Mixing physical exertion with loud music and excited crowds, a dark room, dance music, and someone pushing me to go further—I'm done. I'm toast. I'm so happy. I'm so moved. I'm in heaven. Soul Cycle is my happy place.

It's not everyone's cup of tea—if you're easily overstimulated or overwhelmed, or if being pushed emotionally and physically makes you feel threatened, you're going to want to stay far away from the dark room with the thumping music and the headset-ready instructor who wants to change your life.

I sat there in the room with my dark and bruised-up heart, desperate to move and desperate to be moved by God—searching for Him in a spin class for two significant reasons: (1) I think God can move anywhere and often does, and (2) my church suddenly didn't feel so safe for me. There were no leaders to blame other than myself, and there was nowhere to hide, so I was looking to be led and fed anywhere and everywhere God was willing to show up.

I was listening to sermons, spending hours on my knees, and poring over God's Word for encouragement—but I was also looking for Him on this trip to LA. *Come Father—breathe a fresh wind, bring a fresh fire, do more soul work in me in this short trip than I could ask or imagine. Put the romantic comedy storyline to shame with the renewed sense of purpose You're going to bring. Please.*

I went in needy. And God showed up.

THE WORD OF GOD AGREED

The instructor's name was David, and I can't tell you that he's a Christian. But I can tell you I wouldn't be surprised if he was, because it was 7 a.m. on a Friday, and David straight-up got to work ministering to everyone in the room, including me.

From the moment the doors closed, the lights dimmed, and the volume of the music increased, he started preaching. To be honest, he never got on his bike once—he had a stand-in gal to do the cycling for him so he could use every ounce of his energy to lead us. And as the music pulsed and our feet started pumping, David paced and yelled.

He started the class honoring one rider who just happened to be celebrating her birthday—he had us cheer for her—and then he got more intentional and personal in his affirmation as the class went on.

He started by telling her that joy was her birthright, hope was her birthright, and love was her birthright. He told her that this was a fresh year, a fresh chance to be who she was made to be, to step into her calling and step away from the fears of the past. I was just one bike behind her, and I watched her feet speed up, watched the tears carve paths down her cheeks, watched her nod in agreement with what he was saying. David was giving, she was receiving, and it was beautiful.

But then he turned to the rest of us, and in a loud and emphatic voice, he began assuring us of the same truths! It might not be our birthdays, it might not be a literal new year for us, but it could be the start of something new—we could leave behind the brokenness of our pasts and press into a new season. His words meant more to me than he could have guessed, because I didn't just hear them as general wisdom and empty truths.

The Word of God tucked into my heart agreed with the affirmations this stranger was saying over me. Second Corinthians 5:17 was resounding in my brain: *The old has gone, the new has come!* It was the very first verse I memorized as a believer twenty years ago, and the Lord was bringing it to mind in that very moment, reminding me that the hurt I'd left behind in Charleston didn't have to dictate my future purpose. I was grateful, relieved, and refreshed—so I pedaled faster.

A song began that coincided with a steep climb on our bikes. As it progressed, we were supposed to choose to increase the incline ourselves. If you haven't been to a stationary cycling class, here's how this works: the difficulty of the pedaling is controlled by a small knob on your bike. As you turn it to the right, the resistance increases, simulating a hill. As you turn it to the left, pedaling gets easier. You can feel like you're flying downhill, riding on flat ground, or basically biking up a mountain—you choose by turning the knob and picking your own poison. It's worth it to know that theoretically, you could fake your way through a spin class pretty easily—keeping it turned to low resistance the entire class—but I'm sure you know the saying: you'd only be cheating yourself.

As David encouraged us to keep turning the wheel, to keep pushing against the defeated feeling within us that told us we couldn't, he dropped yet another truth bomb: "You will repeat what you don't repair." He started explaining, again, the universal truth that the wounds for which we don't seek healing will just be replicated over and over in our lives. I thought about my romantic comedy running story, how I'd escaped Charleston just at the pinnacle of my pain, hoping to come back lighter and somehow not caring about all that had been done to me, somehow instinctively able to avoid making the same mistakes over and over again.

Hebrews 12:14–15 from *The Message* (MSG) version of the Bible came to mind:

> Work at getting along with each other and with God. Otherwise you'll never get so much as a glimpse of God. Make sure no one gets left out of God's generosity. Keep a sharp eye out for weeds of bitter discontent. A thistle or two gone to seed can ruin a whole garden in no time.

You will repeat what you don't repair. A thistle or two can ruin the whole garden. God's truth, transcending church walls yet again.

Lord, I thought as I spun faster, *I'm listening. I receive this moment and all that You're bringing to the surface. I'll acknowledge my own pain and even examine it, if growth will come on the other side.*

THE PROBLEM PRESENTED

Gals, I could write a hundred more pages about the wisdom David shared that morning. He just kept going and going and going—affirming, encouraging, gesturing wildly, and shouting eternal promises to my shattered heart. The Holy Spirit inside me was working just as hard as I was pedaling, it seemed, connecting the words of our instructor to the revelation of God's Word that was tucked in my memory. It was line after line of LIFE to my very heavy heart.

The second the class was over, I bolted to my locker, grabbed my phone, and tapped an iPhone screenful of notes.

I typed out all the little nuggets of wisdom and truth that my new friend David had poured into my heart through his words. And then, with my own words just about spilling out of me, I found my husband's name in my contacts and called him, burdened to my core with one idea that had risen to the surface above them all:

Nick? Hey babe. It's me. I just got out of Soul Cycle and I need to tell you about it.

This forty-five-minute spin class I just took? It was more life-giving, more encouraging, and spoke more truth to me than any other Christian event I've ever sat through. I felt like I belonged more than I have in any community of believers, and it seemed like I was challenged more by truth, compelled and called to change more than I ever have been through a book or a sermon or a conversation with a friend.

I met with the Lord in Soul Cycle today, and I'm realizing that people everywhere are getting what they need from God from everyone else BUT believers. Because our church is NOT this encouraging, and our friends who love God do NOT speak life like this.

I'm worried we're missing out on doing what David is doing every single day. And we're in full-time ministry. If we're missing it—how many people are letting the opportunity slip by to change the lives of those around them?

As I confessed my concerns to Nick, I realized they were bigger and deeper than just my concerns for our life, our family, our church.

I'm worried we're missing it.

We're missing our chance because we're too caught up in our own lives and in the fear that we'll do it wrong.

David isn't missing his chance—but maybe I'm missing mine.

And I know thousands of women who may be missing theirs.

THE WORDS WE NEED MOST

Every week for the last few years, typically on Tuesdays, I have an hour-long call with a stranger. I started taking these coaching calls a while ago because it got too hard to answer all the emails I'd get from women who want to use their gifts or get into ministry in some capacity. So I take one call a week. Sometimes this turns into an all-day session with a brave soul who is willing to come be in my actual space here in Charleston. I meet with hopeful writers, women's ministry leaders and volunteers, gals who have a small business idea they'd love to see come to fruition. I meet with single moms who want to start a small group or college students on the brink of entering the working world, desperate to discern their place in the kingdom, I lend advice. I help these women make a game plan, but more than anything I state one message over and over and over again: *You're the girl for the job.*

If I'm meeting with a college student who wants to write to other women about Jesus, I tell her: *you're the girl for the job.*

A newly married gal finds herself unexpectedly pregnant and overwhelmed at the thought of being a mother: *you're the girl for the job.*

Two friends who want to start a local ministry encouraging the women around them: *you're the girls for the job.*

Is it negligent that I tell so many women the same thing?

Is it false hope to spur them on to some spiritual work when I know it may be harder than they think? Shouldn't I be warning them that it may not go the way they want it to?

Well, honestly, I don't think so. I find that most of us are pre-wired with fear, anticipate struggle, and carry a massive amount of doubt about our capacity. And honestly? We're not crazy. Life is HARD. Loving others is MESSY. Very few people are wildly successful, and no one is immune from getting beat up when they're on mission. We aren't crazy for having fears; we're realistic.

And what about our capacity? You know the old adage, "She believed she could, so she did"? I find that for me, just about *nothing* is further from the truth. I know my own natural capacity—it is very, very low. If left to my own devices, I'd watch Netflix and eat dairy-free yogurt all day long. I'd probably never enter into hard conversations or get out of my comfort zone. If I wanted to do things that made me feel capable, things that celebrated my strengths, I'd have a life that consisted of taking naps and making coffee. I'm naturally good at both of those things.

If I worked only based on what I can do well in my own strength, I'd never have children, get married, do ministry, drive a car, write books, love my neighbors, go on vacation, live on mission, serve the homeless, lead a church, start businesses, have friends, or encourage *anyone*. I would never live. I would never love. I would never taste abundance.

So how can I tell women every single week that they're the girl for the job? And what basis do I have for writing an entire book telling you the exact same thing? I'm certain the Holy Spirit was using David and his words that day in the spin class, but what grounds do I have to believe the encouragement that came my way that day? And every time I open the Word of God?

Here's the secret:

We are the girls for the job because of the God of all capacity who not only calls us but equips us, and dwells within us, enabling us to carry out His plans. We are able to live, to love, to move, to repair, to receive, to heal, to hope because of Him. We are the girls for the job, for this season, for this life, for the joy and blessing of those around us at this exact appointed time because God has placed us here. He's called us to be His ambassadors, and He doesn't make mistakes.

THIS IS YOUR INVITATION

This isn't a book about a spin class, and it's honestly not even a book about us. In the name of Jesus, my prayer is that you'll find that every single page of this book is about the God who made us good, set us free, called us holy, invited us on mission, and never wavers in His capability or His capacity. This is a book about the God who is right for the job, and it's an invitation to take your place as His coheir, servant, and friend.

This book won't puff you up and tell you that you have all you need, but it *will* point to the One who does. This book won't beckon you to be blind to your circumstances, but it *will* enlighten you to the truth that you're placed where you're at, with what you've got, on purpose.

We're going to go on a journey, one that I pray will take you to a place of being able to boldly, humbly proclaim that

YOU are the girl for the job—the girl for the task He's given you and the girl for every task He is going to give you in the future. More than that, I hope these words commission you as an ambassador to speak life and authority to those around you, telling them *they* are the girls, boys, men, women, people, children of God for the jobs that He's given them.

We're going to dive into an others-focused mind-set, setting our sights on their good and His glory, and squashing the power of comparison and the feelings of inadequacy in one crushing blow. Partnering with the Holy Spirit, we'll dive back into our pasts, taking stock of where we've been and what He's given us. We'll look at our strengths, our weaknesses, our stories, and the tools we've been handed by a good Father with new eyes—eyes that can see belief and hope.

Next, we'll take God at His Word and ask Him for vision to see what it is He's called us to, not just in the present but for the days and years to come. We won't approach Him as though He's a genie in a bottle or a Magic Eight Ball we can shake to find out the future, and we won't expect Him to provide a detailed plan, but we will look to Scripture for truth and stand firm on the promises that say He'll provide wisdom when we ask and that He'll tell us to go to the right or to the left (see James 1:5 and Isaiah 30:21, respectively).

This is our invitation to strip off defeat, kick fear in the actual face, and get over ourselves so we can get on with living the wild and wonderful mission that He has for our lives. We're going to bring the scariest parts of stepping into our calling into the light, to let Him shine on them, exposing the lies that keep us hiding in the dark. Friends, while reading this book we're going to make a plan, and then, in the name of Jesus, we're going to begin making *moves* that align with His call on our lives. We're not just going to affirm that we're the girls for the job; we're going to agree with our actions.

This is your invitation. This is our invitation. It is for those of us who are burdened and broken, beat up by the sin of others and the inadequacies of our own lives. It is for those of us who took a break when it got too hard, and it is for those of us who never took the first step because it was too scary. This is an invitation for the women of God who have been stepping into the call of God on their lives for years to keep going, to keep fighting.

This is an invitation to not miss it, to not miss out on the thrilling and heart-wrenching life of love that God has for us. Because I don't believe David should get to have all the fun. And I don't believe we want to live in a world where a spin class speaks more truth than a sisterhood of women who have taken God at His Word to rise up and love with all we've got.

This book is for you. It's your invitation to leave behind defeat and disbelief and to permanently believe that God is who He says He is and that because of this, you are exactly who He's made you to be, on purpose.

You're the girl for the job. If you're ready to get to work, keep reading.

CALL IT QUITS

It's time we quit arguing with God about our
inadequacy and start relying on His
capacity.

CHAPTER 1

IT'S QUITTING TIME

I'll never forget the day I decided I wasn't all that pretty.

It was early in my freshman year of college, a bright fall day, and I was walking from my class to the dorm. This first semester of college I'd taken all morning classes, as I was attempting to get school finished early in the day, work a part-time job in the afternoon, and study or hang with friends in the evening. Fall in South Carolina means it's still unthinkably warm, so I was walking and sweating and hadn't attempted to dress nicely or put on makeup. I felt great about that decision as the perspiration just dripped down my face and neck, pooling into a moist spot between my shoulders.

And then I saw her.

She had short, dark, straight hair that hit just at her shoulders in a beautifully natural way. Her outfit was similar to mine, just somehow better: a T-shirt and shorts, tennis shoes, and minimal jewelry. But her face was like something Michelangelo would choose for a muse—her bone structure was flawless, and I wondered how cheeks could be so pointy and pretty all at once. Her olive skin was tight, as though someone had pulled it back and tied it with string beneath her hair. Even her eyes sparkled—*literally sparkled*—as I passed her, me on my way to the dorm, she on her way to wherever impossibly beautiful people go.

Sixteen years later, I can still describe the face of the girl who convinced me I wasn't all that pretty. I can still see her in my mind's eye. For all I can remember, I don't think I ever saw her again, but if she walked into a restaurant here in present-day Charleston, I'm almost positive I could ID her in a second.

That was the moment when I first thought to myself that some people just have beauty naturally. That thought has stayed with me for sixteen years.

My kind of beauty, on the other hand, is the *un*natural kind. Some people look stellar in their husband's sweats with no makeup on. When I don't wear makeup (which is roughly four out of seven days of the week), everyone asks if I'm tired/depressed/sick/okay. I can't fit into my husband's sweats because he's super fit and trim, and while I get after it in the gym, too, my hips and booty are about twice the size of his, so we can just throw out that scenario altogether. My hair started going gray in my late twenties, but not in a distinguished way. We're talking squirrely, wiry, disobedient wildfires of gray that sprout up all along my part, so I dye those suckers regularly.

Don't misunderstand me—I feel *great* about how God made me, but I am *not* what you'd describe as a natural beauty. It takes about forty-five minutes on average for me to look my best, and that doesn't mean I actually spend forty-five minutes getting ready every day. I'm just down with not looking my best most days because it's my quiet rebellion against the confines and constructs of our society that say women can't be useful unless they're flawless.

But back to that day during my freshman year in college: my perspective shifted because I realized that, on the natural beauty scale, I would essentially never rank. But here's what I want you to catch: I wasn't devastated or dismayed. On the contrary, it was as if a fresh wave of freedom passed over me when I realized I was out of the running.

OR THAT GREAT OF A MOTHER

I became a mom in a season where most of my friends were still in college, much less thinking about marriage or starting families. I was twenty-one when I got pregnant, had been married for eight months, and honestly, I didn't even slightly mind being the one in my group of friends to go first. My oldest child is now rounding the corner to twelve years old, and half my friends still don't have kids. But I *love* that we share our lives with people in diverse stages of life and always have. Our kiddos have grown up with the best spiritual aunts and uncles—single or newly married friends who have the margin and passion to invest in them—but what they don't have is a plethora of play-dates, since we don't spend time exclusively with other families who have kids our age.

My first child was born into a community where we were literally the only people our age having children, but we made a move (across the country) to Seattle just before our second was born. Then we had our third baby just a year after the second. So we were twenty-four and twenty-five with three children under three, living literally as far as we could be (while staying in America) from our families. God provided abundant community quickly—friends who are still some of our closest to date, and to top it off, they were all our age and having kids quickly, like us.

You know what happens when you go from being the only mom in her young twenties to being one in a crowd? Or, moreover, when the crowd you're in is filled with women who've always dreamed of being mothers? They all made their own baby food, talked about homeschooling, and wore their babies in slings. These were essentially *professional moms*. They knew so much more about the whole enterprise than I ever could. And the kids?! The kids were like baby geniuses. How could they not be, with wildly intentional mothers speaking life and hope and learning into them all day?

My motherhood plan was essentially this: *wing it*. We did a lot of baby food in plastic containers and PBS up until that point. Not being around other mothers had allowed me to live in the dark, oblivious to the horrible phenomenon termed the "Mommy Wars," but suddenly my eyes were opened. There *was* a competition, and I was incredibly behind.

Not sure what I mean? Think about this in your community: *Who is the cute mom?* You know, the one who always looks good and whose kids always look good. You've mentioned it to her, or maybe you only say it when she's not there. *Which one is the healthy mom?* Her kids have the most nutritious snacks, and you won't catch an ounce of plastic anywhere near them. *Who's the mom with the vibrant marriage?* Everyone is so impressed because they still make it on regular date nights or anniversary getaways. They're so in love! Motherhood hasn't fazed her!

For whatever reason, motherhood brings the race to be the

best to the surface like no other. And we unknowingly partner with it when we label and even laud one another. In all three books I've written, I've talked about my friend Karen in some way, shape, or form because she really is one of the wisest and most pure-hearted friends I have. And she is an *incredible* mom, mostly because she somehow constantly rises above what is expected of her and just does what God tells her to do.

But one day I was with a crew of women, most of whom don't have children, who were privately praising Karen and her motherhood in a way that made me uncomfortable. It wasn't jealousy; I took myself out of the running to be the best mom years ago. What messed with me was that I was hearing their acclaim with fresh ears—I was hearing how much pressure we put on one another to be perfect.

"She's so calm!"

"She literally *never* yells."

"She's so creative!"

"She's read so many books, and she's always reading to her girls."

I loved Karen enough to want these women to see the best in her, even if she *did* yell, even if she *lost her chill*, even if she ran out of things to do with her kids and stuck them in front of a Disney movie for an afternoon. I wanted them to see that Karen was an incredible mom, the absolute best mom for the job, because she was the one God had given to those girls *on purpose*. And what made her motherhood so life-giving to watch was this one thing: *she believed she was the girl for the job*. It wasn't because she was spinning her wheels trying to be her best; it was because she was resting on His strength and just shining where He placed her.

As I said, I had to take myself out of the running for the contest of best mom years ago. I don't remember exactly when it happened, I only know that I don't ever want to be back in the race. God showed me that when I am trying to be the best mom in the eyes of everyone else, the people who lose are the ones I'm trying to mother. There's a choice to pursue the prize for the best (through likes on social media, the approval of my peers, or meeting some arbitrary standard of perfection) or to be present, and I often choose incorrectly. When I love my kids—specifically, how they *need* to be loved, to the glory of God and for the praise of no one else—it might not look all that sparkly to the outside world. But that's okay, because I'm the girl for the *unique job of mothering my own children,* not the winner of the best mom race. I've taken myself out of the running. And I've never known so much freedom.

LET'S QUIT NOW

You may not care a thing about beauty, and motherhood might not be on your radar. I realize these are easy examples for some of us to relate to and easy for others of us to dismiss. But it doesn't change the undeniable truth that somewhere in your life, there is temptation to measure up, to compete, to stand out, to rank. Where in your life do you feel a constant or frequent desire to look to the left or the right and compare yourself to others? Maybe you'd never admit you're trying to be the best, but quietly you're spinning your wheels. You might never dream of saying it out loud to another human, but you're silently exploring where you rank at _____.

Maybe you picked up this book out of that need, out of that desire to rise to the top or, at the very least, to find the confidence to begin running at all. Maybe you grabbed it because you're in need of the world's biggest spiritual pep talk or because no one has ever equated you with being able, special, fruitful, or appointed.

If so, I'm sorry to tell you that at the very beginning of this book, *the very first thing I'm going to ask you to do is quit. Give up. Surrender.*

In the race to be the best woman.
The best servant.
The most authentic.
The most hospitable.
The most encouraging.
The most studious.
The most creative.
The best mom.
The most energetic.
The best listener.
The most effortlessly put together.
The most successful small business owner.
The funniest.
The best wife.
The most empathetic.
The most justice-minded.
The fittest.
The most capable.
The cleanest.
The cutest.

The most self-sufficient.
The best leader.
The most quiet.
The healthiest.
The most fun and spontaneous.
The most positive.
The best friend.
The most productive.

Whatever it is for you, whatever goal or attribute or personality characteristic you've decided is important for you to master, even maybe to excel in, passing those around you, I'm going to ask you to quit it. And here are a couple of reasons why:

We cannot seek God's glory and our own at the same time. If any part of our hearts is divided, seeking to win rather than seeking to wonder at His goodness, let's just quit right now.

We can't seek to be the girl for the job and the girl who wins at the same time. You are the girl for the job, and I'm going to spend the rest of this book telling you why we can biblically stand on that truth, unpacking how we can actively obey the call He's given us. But we can't go forward trying to win the award for any of those things mentioned above while we seek to be obedient to what He's particularly called us to.

Our Father in heaven, He's the best, He's the ultimate, and He's here for His glory. Because He calls us, we do have a race to run. But it's not *our* race. It's not a race in which we win the prize and claim the glory for ourselves. It's *His* race, aimed at bringing as many people under the light and life of His love as possible.

Therefore we also, since we are surrounded by so great a cloud of witnesses, let us lay aside every weight, and the sin which so easily ensnares us, and let us run with endurance the race that is set before us, looking unto Jesus, the author and finisher of our faith, who for the joy that was set before Him endured the cross, despising the shame, and has sat down at the right hand of the throne of God. (Hebrews 12:1–2 NKJV)

The first breaking, burdensome weight we're going to have to lay aside to love well is the desire to be the best. So let's give up now. Let's quit. *Let's take ourselves out of the running.* I'm going to spend the rest of the book making a case to convince you that you're the girl for the job. But truly: it's God's job, God's strength, God's power, and God's grace that actually get the work done. To step into this truth, to take our rightful place in this narrative, we've got to take ourselves out of the running for His job and take ourselves out of any race that pits us against other people or ourselves. To start, we've got to quit.

CHAPTER 2

LET'S TALK ABOUT YOUR IDEAL SELF

*C*an you scoot to the side so I can open the fridge?"
A few years ago, I was standing with my husband in our
tiny galley kitchen while he was cooking, catching up on the
events of the day. Now, in our new home, I can climb on top of
the countertops and sit while Nick cooks and we talk. But our
last kitchen was so tiny, I just had to stand there, awkwardly
ducking out of his way when he needed a pot or a pan or to
get into the fridge. This kitchen scenario works for us because
Nick is a phenomenal cook, and he loves to take the reins in
the kitchen. His only request is that I hang out with him while
he cooks and that we use that time to catch up on our days.

On that long-ago day in the old galley kitchen, though, my
phone was plugged into an outlet on the tiny counter all the way
at the back of the kitchen, next to the garage door, and I could
see it buzzing and lighting up, but I couldn't get to it. Nconn
(what I call him) is one of those phenomenal humans who is
really good at being in the moment, and while he always knows

where his phone is, he doesn't feel the need to be able to check it. He's content to leave text messages unread for hours, and he does the responsible thing and only opens emails when he knows he has the mental margin to answer them immediately.

I'm more like a rabid squirrel when it comes to technology, and I'm not proud of it! My phone generally lives in my back pocket or right hand, and when a text message buzzes, I will shuffle to see it and answer it with an eagerness that all but screams, *"A friend! A friend! I love my friends!"*

But when Nick is cooking and we're catching up on our day, I try to play it cool and follow his lead. I do my best to be totally in the moment, ignoring the flashing screen and keeping my gaze on his steely blue eyes. Which are not bad to be focused on, you know what I'm saying?

So I could see my phone buzzing, six feet away, beyond Nick and the amazing dinner he was making for our family, and my curiosity was piqued. *Stay in the moment*, my brain screamed to my heart, until finally Nick caught my gaze and said, "You've got a text, want to answer it?"

Thank you, God, for a man who loves me just as I am, not interested in cooking and happily connected to technology. In Jesus' name, amen.

I skittered across the kitchen as he continued working. When I got to my phone, I was thrilled to see a message from my friend Jessica. Jessica is a gem—everyone who knows her loves her, and it's easy to know why.

Jessica Honegger is an incredibly successful business-woman, an author, and a podcast host, and she loves Jesus vibrantly and wildly. I love talking business and gleaning wisdom from Jessica, but more than that, I love praying with her—listening to her talk to God, agreeing with what she is saying, and thanking God that we're sisters in Christ.

Anyway, the text was from Jessica. She was inviting me to her family's ranch house for a few days that coming summer, to meet with her and other businesswomen, authors, and ministry leaders. She rattled off the names of the other women who would be attending, and I literally laughed out loud. *One of these things is not like the other*, I thought. I was just me, messy Jess in her galley kitchen, pretending like I knew what I was doing as I fumbled my way through my first few published books and online businesses. I would go on to tell a few friends who was invited to Jessica's leadership retreat, and a few of them would bravely agree, saying, "You seem a little out of place in that bunch."

But not Nick. I read the text to him and told him how insecure I felt about going on a leadership retreat with such accomplished and successful women—and he said, "No— you're the girl for the job. God's invited you to this. Go and give what you've got, and take what you can. We don't ascribe to or live by the hierarchy of worldly success or labels anyhow, so who says you're not qualified to be there? Go! Learn! Enjoy! Say 'Thank you for inviting me, of course I'll be there!'"

And that's how I found myself on a ranch in June 2015 with some astoundingly fruitful women—baring my soul and working through the yuckiest and heaviest parts of my heart: the stuff that was holding me back from stepping into all God had asked me to do.

We spent the weekend working through one worksheet that broke our personalities down into different categories. My favorite category was the one called "Your Idealized Self."

We learned over the weekend that all of the parts are important (I glossed over this important detail) and that integrating all the facets of our selves would maximize our leadership potential.

Your Ideal Self is you thriving at the height of who God made you to be. It's you on your absolute best day, with no obstacles or barriers. It's a real part of how you were created, but it's obviously not the complete picture. But I got hung up on the Ideal Self because I already know her through and through, in and out, backwards and forwards. I'm well acquainted with her, and I really, really wish she showed up more frequently.

Here's a definition from a psychology glossary that unpacks a little more about the Ideal Self: *The Ideal Self is an idealized version of yourself created out of what you have learned from your life experiences, the demands of society, and what you admire in your role models.* I'd take it a step further and say that as women of God, we know that all knowledge and vision originate from God, and that He uses it as a helpful tool for us to partner with the Holy Spirit this way and see what can truly be.

I think, in a lot of ways, when we imagine our ideal selves, we're not just dreaming about who we *could* be, we're exploring part of who God *made us* to be. We're opening up the boundaries that used to hold us back and seeing our potential with His eyes.

What about you? Have you ever thought about your Ideal Self? Have you ever dreamed about her or imagined what she can accomplish? Also, isn't it interesting how our ideal for our own lives changes as we grow? One year, your Ideal Self might be a powerful, independent businesswoman, and a few years later, you may picture her as a stay-at-home mom with a dozen kids.

Would you take a moment now and think about her? Ideal You? You at your absolute best? You without limits or weaknesses? You without a lack of belief, without fears or concerns? Picture her—maybe write a paragraph and describe her. I dare you! If Christ is in you, so is the power of the Holy Spirit, so don't go telling me you're not imaginative or creative. The God who created color, the cosmos, every majestic mountain and beautiful flower and powerful storm made you in His image, so I know you can do this. Meet your ideal gal before you meet mine, and then we'll come back together.

MEET IDEAL JESS

I meet with my Ideal Self once a week. We basically have a standing date. I prepare for it, I look forward to it, and if I'm not careful, I spend the rest of the week craving to be back in her presence. My weekly date with Ideal Jess is every Monday at 8 a.m., so preparation starts the evening before. I eat a healthy meal for dinner on Sunday night because I'm trying not to be gassy or bloated when it's time to hang out with her. I'm careful to choose an outfit on Monday morning that makes me feel free and confident because I don't want to be distracted by insecurity over my clothing during this appointment.

As I drive the kids to school on Monday morning, I'm gentler than usual with them because I can't go into my meeting with Ideal Jess feeling busted for barking on the way.

After dropping them off, I pick up a venti black coffee from Starbucks—I always tip because Ideal Jess is so stinking generous, and I'm almost with her, so I might as well begin to act like her. I make my way from downtown Charleston, leaving behind the Monday morning hustle, and drive over the beautiful bridge that connects the city to the suburbs and then the next bridge, smaller and less regal, but still majestic for one incredible reason. This second, smaller bridge takes me to the beach—Sullivan's Island, to be exact. I turn left at the main intersection, which has only a stop sign, and make my way a few blocks down to Station 19.

I park, leaving my phone in the car, and as I step out I can feel the breeze and smell the salt air. It's time for my weekly prayer walk, which means it's Ideal Jess time.

My sneakers seek out the hard-packed sand, and I start stomping my way down the beach. I try to pause and just listen, then I start praising God and thanking Him for what I've seen of Him that week. I speak out loud because it helps me stay connected to my Father best. I tell Him what I need help with and where I could really use His encouragement. There is more listening and pausing. There is arm waving and arm pumping, there is gesturing, and sometimes there is a brief pause to stand firm and raise both hands in worship. Sometimes there are tears. As I round the corner of Sullivan's Island that points back toward downtown Charleston, I sit on the rocks and watch my city. I pray for her, ask God for her good. And then I walk back, doing much of the same.

See, it's really a meeting with God, but it's Ideal Jess who shows up for that encounter. She's Ideal Jess because she's not actively sinning, she's not getting frustrated with anyone, she's not standing in the mirror wondering why her hips are uneven, and she isn't engaging with fear or doubt or shame. She's me, at my best, in the throne room of grace, doing what I was made to do. Or so I thought.

I came back from Jessica's retreat and felt so affirmed by the concept of Ideal Jess, motivated to spend more time with her, *as* her. Then, one day I was catching up my mom, sharing all that I'd learned, when she said something shocking, jarring, and incredibly wise that stopped me in my tracks.

As I told my mom about Ideal Jess, I watched her expression move from open to closed, her lips drawing together into a tight line as I talked. It was evident she still wanted to hear me out, but she was skeptical about what I was saying. Finally the words bubbled to the surface. "But that's not really who you are," she said. "I mean it *is*, but it's not the whole picture."

My loving and crazy-wise mom went on to bring back the main message of the leadership conference (which I had overlooked in my enthusiasm over Ideal Jess) as she explained that the way she saw me was much more comprehensive. It included Ideal Jess on the beach, but it also included Jess the mom in the middle of a messy house on a busy day. It included Jess ministering to people, often imperfectly, receiving grace from God and others. My mom's picture of me even included Jessi, the slightly chubby eleven-year-old version of me who liked to hide in the rec room, eating bagels away from the world. She saw the whole me: wounds, hopes, healed places, hurts, strengths, weaknesses, and victory all in one, and she wanted me to see all of it as good, all of it as usable by God.

She was right.

YOUR IDEAL SELF IS NOT WHO YOU THINK

My mom knew what the leadership retreat leaders knew because it's a universal truth found in the Word of God.

My Ideal Self, even though she's super spiritual and spends a lot of time praying, is innocuous because she's fragile—she's like a sandcastle that crumbles when other people are around. She is unreliable and unattainable because she's not *real* in the way that characters and personalities formed over time and through trouble are real. There's no trouble coming her way; there's nothing she must persevere against; it's just her and the ocean and her waving hands having the time of her life.

My Ideal Self isn't all that powerful because she isn't complete without the other people who push her to her limits— the kids who annoy her sometimes, but who also ignite her passion and fortitude. The husband who can hurt her, leaving her exposed and insecure like no one else, but who also has the capacity to commission her like no other because he sees her at her worst and encourages her to keep ministering anyhow. Ideal Jess on the beach on a Monday morning isn't completely able to stand because she's flimsy without the positioning of her past mistakes and failures holding her up and teaching her where *not* to go again.

I could go on and on. But let's get back to you. Remember that picture of your Ideal Self you described or contemplated? I know, she's *amazing*, right? She's got this. She's on top of things. She's intentional, purposeful, grounded, prepared.

But here's the kicker, here's the crazy news:

Ideal You, she's not nearly as strong as *Actual* You. See, she doesn't make mistakes, so she doesn't have to rise up after falling down. She doesn't have self-imposed or world-inflicted limits, so she doesn't have to push past them in the name of Jesus. Fear isn't on her radar, so faith doesn't have to be either. Don't throw her in the trash or leave her behind, because she is a part of you. She is the beautiful, Spirit-filled part that listens to the Lord about what could be ahead. But she is not nearly as impactful or interesting or impressive—mostly because she's not actually *here*.

You, the broken you, the messy you, the you filled with past regrets and mistakes—you're the girl for the job. You, the one who sins and experiences grace, the one who feels fear and chooses faith, the one who hurts and can be hurt—you're the girl for the job. You, the interruptible. You, the unexchange-able. You, the complete-picture version of a woman created by the God who formed the universe with intention, talent, creativity, glory, and His perfect power—*you* are the girl for the job. You, placed right where you're at—in this season, around these people, with all the tools you need to love them and continually point them to Jesus—*you* are the girl for the job.

Your Ideal Self: she's got nothing on you.

ACTUAL YOU IS A POTENTIAL POWERHOUSE

I love it when I find a Bible verse I've never read before that moves me. I read it over and over again, marveling at how creative and honest God is to put such helpful and resounding wisdom in the Bible. And I also love Bible verses that bring power in different seasons, and even when I expect that they might lose their weight over time, they never do.

Second Corinthians 12:9 is one of those verses for me. If we actually believe it's true, it gives us some knowledge about God that is so wild and counteractive to the ways of this world. It brings hope, comfort, peace, and wild worship to my heart—no matter the circumstances of my life.

> But he said to me, "My grace is sufficient for you, for my power is made perfect in weakness." Therefore I will boast all the more gladly about my weaknesses, so that Christ's power may rest on me. (2 Corinthians 12:9)

Science-y left turn coming your way. Hydrogen by itself is an incredibly dangerous material—it's highly flammable, it's explosive, and it causes asphyxiation in humans because it leaches the oxygen and the ability to breathe right from them. Hydrogen *plus* oxygen, on the other hand, forms the most refreshing and valuable liquid on earth: water. Hydrogen will kill us; hydrogen plus oxygen keeps us alive.

I understand that Actual You has weaknesses, that she has experienced unimaginable pain and heartache. Unfortunately, I also know that in her lifetime, she's probably also caused a lot of pain, and she's sinned against God and the people she loves. She can say hurtful things, do hurtful things, and she's had countless hurtful things done to her. There are lies she's been told by others and by the enemy of her soul; there are wounds she has received that run deep and cut to the quick. Actual You has the capacity to walk around the world wounded and wounding, doing more damage than hydrogen could ever dream of.

But Actual You *plus* grace . . . Actual You *combined* with

49

the mercy, kindness, restoration, and resurrection power of Jesus Christ our Savior? She is spiritual water. She is life embodied. She's the representative picture of the gospel that the angels *wish* they could experience, walking around on earth. The verse that tells me that, 1 Peter 1:12 (MSG), says this: "Do you realize how fortunate you are? Angels would have given anything to be in on this!" For everything I can gather about angels, here's what I surmise: their choice is to worship God for eternity or not; they don't get to live in the in-between of daily grace, the way we do. There is not an actualized and gospel-receiving version of life available for them. *That power and purpose is reserved just for us.*

Here's what I believe with absolutely all that I've got: You are the girl for the job. You're the one God has placed right where you're at with His perfect knowledge and foresight. It has taken one million—maybe one zillion (who knows?)—slight moves of His hand to place you in this exact moment. All of the small and ordinary miracles that had to occur at just the right time for you to be born, for you to stay alive and well, for you to be introduced to God or this book—whichever came first—are Him. For you to know the exact people you know, to have had the exact experiences you've had—all Him. You are the girl for the job: what you've got inside of you is what He has perfectly ordained for you to use for His glory.

But your Ideal Self? She doesn't have what it takes. She can't love like you; she doesn't have your failures or weaknesses to ground her in the grace of the gospel. She doesn't have the hope that springs up in the darkest times, and she doesn't know grace like you and I do. No one has to forgive her, so she doesn't know how to receive grace, and because she lives in some alternate reality where there is no tension, she can't press in and press through like you.

You're going to have to thank her for who she is and what God uses her to tell you. You're going to have to acknowledge that she's already a large part of who you are—all of her strengths and glory and power are found in the resurrection power of the cross, and you've got access to those, too. But then you've got to say goodbye to her. You've got to stop pretending to *be* her. You've got to stop wishing you could be her. Your Ideal Self is not your most influential self. Your Ideal Self is *not* the girl for the job. You are.

CHAPTER 3

HE IS THE HERO, YOU ARE THE RESCUE PLAN

July 23, 2005 was the hottest day on record in Charleston, South Carolina, for the whole year.

It was my wedding day, so the weather is emblazoned in my mind forever. And it was the heat that marked the handful of minutes leading up to me walking down the aisle. Those minutes are etched in my brain, and I often replay them, running my mind's eye along their bumps, curves, and jagged edges.

The backstory is this: I wasn't entirely sure I wanted anyone to walk me down the aisle. It wasn't a power play or a declaration of independence for me; it's just that I have *two* great dads (biological and stepdad). I didn't want either one to feel slighted since they'd both played such different and vital roles in my life. So the plan was a solo walk, until I toured the church we'd get married in a month or so before the wedding. I stood at the back of the church and I knew I'd need *someone* back there to hold my hand. The gravity of that moment was too intense, and I didn't want to be alone.

So we planned a combination: my biological dad walking me down the aisle and my stepdad meeting us at the altar. Flash forward a few weeks, and it was all happening.

A few minutes earlier, in true wild wedding fashion, I'd had the first nosebleed of my entire life, when I was already wearing my dress, seemingly brought on by what? We didn't know. The heat? The stress? The dehydration because I was all hopped up on Diet Coke and coffee and hadn't seen a glass of water in days? (The early 2000s were a different time; don't judge me.) The nosebleed had come and gone quickly, my dress was fine, and my dad and I were standing behind the thick wooden doors. I could hear the music swelling inside the sanctuary and people rustling due to the excessive warmth permeating their tuxes, fussy dresses, and suit jackets.

Dad turned to me with tears in his eyes as he opened his palm and showed me a seashell hidden in his travel-worn tanned hands. He'd found it on the beach earlier that day, and there was something he wanted to tell me. I could see his mouth moving; I watched his lips quiver and the tears slowly drip from the corner of each eye, watched him brush them away with a slight flick of his finger. He was saying something wild, precious, and meaningful, but for the life of me, *I couldn't hear him*, and to this day I can't tell you what in the world he was talking about.

What I *could* hear was an incredibly loud and banal inner monologue that was screaming, *DID WE GET ALL THE BLOOD OFF MY FACE? IS ANY OF IT STUCK IN MY NOSE HAIRS?* I'm massively ashamed to admit that I interrupted him halfway through his emotive and beautiful monologue and asked him to check me one more time before the doors opened. "Any more blood? Any makeup smeared? Thank you for the seashell. Let's go!"

I missed the moment. I was twenty when I got married and hadn't yet developed the emotional maturity it takes to savor a moment like that one. It would take me a few more years to acquire the ability to stay present even when it makes me uncomfortable. I didn't yet know the value of keeping eye contact, leaving room for the awkward silence, or how to allow the tension of an occasion teach me something.

So to be completely transparent, I missed *a lot* of moments that month. It's a funny story to tell about the ignorance of youth and the stress of wedding days, but now, thirteen years later, I'd give a million dollars to go back and just hear whatever it was my dad was about to say. On top of that, I'd give another million to have the capacity to go back into the moment, rip every last bobby pin from my head (who could think straight like that?), tousle my hair, take my shoes off, and repeat my walk down the aisle toward the man I was about to marry.

Because instead of doing that, just after I brushed off my dad's incredibly sentimental gift, I did a kind of strange, strained rendition of a walk toward the front of the sanctuary. Due to the excessive hairpins and the particular way I was holding my bouquet so as not to create the dreaded "back fat" when I moved my arms, I looked less like a serene bride and more like a stilted mannequin who was determined to move the muscles in her feet and nothing else. Of course, hindsight tells me *now* that the twenty-year-old who was living on bran muffins and Diet Coke had nothing that even resembled fat on her posterior (and boy, have things changed), but alas, we can't go back and recreate moments, can we?

I missed the moment because my focus was on the wrong things. I'm still married, it was just one day, and there's obviously grace, but the regret I feel is a helpful tool that tells me the way I responded in that moment truly mattered, I missed it, and there was a consequence.

I love my dad, and I obviously love my husband, but it's not only that I regret missing moments with *them*. What I lost by making myself the focal point in those sweeping, grand, glorious snapshots of life was having my heart and spirit attuned to what *God* was doing. The ancient Celts came up with the phrase "thin places" to describe moments or physical spaces where heaven and earth collapse in on one another and become indistinguishable. One of my favorite authors, Shauna Niequist, describes them in her book *Bittersweet*:

> Thin places: places where the boundary between the divine world and the human world becomes almost nonexistent, and the two, divine and human, can for a moment, dance together uninterrupted. Some are physical places, and some aren't places at all, but states of being or circumstances or seasons.*

Weddings, the day a baby is born, holidays, first dates, funerals, even the day you're fired or your best friend betrays you: it seems these are the days when the Spirit of God is soaking into every breath, conversation, and blink in a much more palpable way. We can see His hand moving, we can see His heart beating as He meets us where we're at in the thin places.

---

* Shauna Niequist, *Bittersweet: Thoughts on Change, Grace, and Learning the Hard Way* (Grand Rapids, MI: Zondervan, 2013), 92.

Did God want to heal some broken parts of my heart regarding my earthly father just before he attempted to give away what I felt he'd given away prematurely years before? Did He want to teach me about kingdom beauty through the seashell story just before I paraded myself as a beacon of attempted attractiveness through a crowd of my most loved friends and family? Was the Holy Spirit going to give me a word of promise or a vision for my marriage, for my future husband, as I walked down the aisle, my eyes locked to his?

Did my heavenly Father have something planned that was better than I could ask or imagine, that He'd accomplish by the power of the Holy Spirit, right there in that sanctuary by the sea? *I vote yes.* Did I miss it because I was worried about errant streaks of blood that were nowhere to be found and back fat that is now laughable? *Also yes.* Is there grace for me? Am I still married, and do I still have a relationship with my dad? *One hundred percent yes.*

But I missed the moment, an inevitable divine and holy intervention, because I made it all about myself. By God's grace, we get to learn from our pasts and learn from one another and plant flags in the front yards of our hearts that wave this banner in bright colors and bold words: *I refuse to miss out on what God is doing, what He might be saying, and how He may be miraculously intervening. I refuse to miss out because I'm focused on myself, my insecurities, or my perception of my own capacity.*

THE RESCUE IS ON THE WAY

Let's walk through a small part of the story of the Israelites, God's chosen people of the Old Testament. Their story starts much earlier than we will—we're just deep diving into one snap-shot. In Genesis 45, we learn that Joseph saved his brothers, who had sold him into slavery, when the country experienced an extreme famine. God warned Joseph about the famine through a dream, instructed him how to take care of everyone. Included in that "everyone" were his traitorous brothers, whom he forgave and to whom he offered refuge. Joseph lived in Egypt when he rescued his brothers, so they set up shop in Egypt as well.

You might say that Joseph, in this case, did *not* miss his moment to be used by God. He could have made it all about himself and denied his brothers safety and security, but he didn't, and his obedience led to them all staying alive and well. In fact, they didn't *just* stay alive and well, but their family grew and grew until it was no longer just one family that the Egyptians allowed to live in their land, but a burgeoning people group that was rapidly growing and making the leaders nervous. This, of course, was long after Joseph and his brothers were dead. The pharaoh, or king, of Egypt was so threatened by these Israelites (Joseph's dad, Jacob, was renamed "Israel" by God, by the way; that's where they got their moniker) that he enslaved them and forced them to work under horrifying conditions.

But the Israelites were incredibly resilient, and the oppression only made them multiply faster and grow stronger, which of course made the Egyptians even *more* fearful of them and in turn led to Pharaoh declaring that all the Israelite baby boys must be killed.

This is one of the parts of the Bible that really gets to me, because I read it not as allegory, but as the history of God moving amongst people—I read it with the belief that it actually happened. And as a mom and a lover of humanity, I feel sick to my stomach when I read that one human was so obsessed with his own power that he ordered babies to be killed at birth by their midwives or literally thrown into the river. But that is exactly what Pharaoh commanded, and for the purpose of where we're headed, I think it's wildly important that we hold the weight of that for a moment.

Human tragedy and extreme social injustice are not new, and even when they have occurred in the past, I believe the devastating pain of others deserves our grief. But here's one snapshot of the Bible I appreciate seeing: the underweaving and working of God's rescue plan, like looking at the back of a tapestry. When we are forced to confront extreme inequality and oppression, we wonder, "Where is God?" The book of Exodus tells us that God was fully engaged, using *humans* as the catalysts, the agents of change, that resulted in rescue. God was broken, devastated over the sin that would lead people to annihilate one another, over the breaking of His chosen people. Where is God in the midst of oppression? I believe He's often working miracles on behalf of His people—miracles we couldn't dream of or see, and He is also stirring, calling, and equipping His people to meet the needs and fight for justice on behalf of their fellow humans. Our Father was not and is not inactive in times of injustice, but rather He is carefully and intentionally using His favorite tool to activate justice: His people. We may feel like we're the ones doing all the work, assuming He is quietly sitting by, when truly, He's the author of justice and we're made in His image—made able by Him to do His work and love His people. No, God's not idle—He is just working a plan that allows us to be a part of the rescue.

And this is the kind of story we find in the book of Exodus— the story of the Israelites, the story of Moses.

Moses was born in the midst of extreme oppression and injustice, during the season when Pharaoh was forcing midwives to kill babies on the brink of birth or to throw them into the Nile River. Specifically, they were killing all the male babies, since, in their patriarchal culture, women carried no threat. As we walk a little further into Moses' story, there are two important observations we can make along the way— observations that only make this moment in Scripture more meaningful for us:

1. Patriarchy and sexism and the enemy of our souls may discount women, but God never did and never does. In fact, He invited many women to rise to the occasion and be His coworkers in the fight against injustice in this story. Pharaoh ordered that all the baby boys be killed, but he made the fatal error of discounting the power of God amongst the women who would rise up and fight against Him. The midwives fought by disobeying his law, Moses' mother fought by hiding her son, Moses' sister fought by strategizing his rescue, and God even used Pharaoh's daughter's gift of mercy to save the man who would come to represent God's power over Egypt. *Big mistake, Pharaoh. Big mistake, Satan.* Culture can discount women, but our God never will.

2. We see some beautiful foreshadowing to another man, born in the midst of injustice, protected by women (and men) so he could lead and love with all He had. Only this time, roughly 1,500 years later, those protecting the boy would be fleeing *to* Egypt instead of away from it.

Early on in the life of Jesus, an angel came to Joseph, warning him to flee with Mary and Jesus to Egypt and remain there until it was safe because Herod sought to kill the promised Christ child. Joseph did as the angel commanded, leaving town in the middle of the night, and they stayed in Egypt until Herod died. (This is recounted for us in Matthew 2.)

Where is God when His people are hurting? Where is God when abuse and persecution are leaning in on all sides? He is executing rescue operations, using ordinary people at every step. We call them the heroes, and we perceive them to be special when, in all actuality, they're just fallible and feeble individuals like us. Their willingness, however reluctant, makes them seem majestic in our eyes—it makes them seem otherworldly and untouchable. Presidents, world leaders, diplomats, authors, speakers, humanitarians, artists, heroes, stars, and explorers. If we're not careful, we can look at their work and misplace them as the target of our worship and reverence. But it has always been Him, always God, beckoning and calling and equipping normal people—even those of us who are reluctant to practice simple obedience—so that the rescue plan can have human hands on it.

Make no mistake: God can work through the supernatural. He can work through the wind and the waves, and He can make the rocks cry out or make the animals talk if we stay silent. But He chooses to use those who are made in His image, the flesh and blood and fallible kids that He loves to partner with as He fights injustice and oppression. Make no mistake that He wants to use you—*you*—to fight the darkness that lives both within and outside of your comfortable boundaries. Make no mistake that we're still in the midst of rescue, that He is still in the process of setting things right. Let's not make the mistake of missing it because our eyes are focused on ourselves, or because they're overwhelmed by the size of the fight, or because we're waiting for a hero to do the work for us.

Although he had wild moments of obedience and faith, Moses almost missed it. And his lack of focus and faith cost him dearly.

MISSING FRUIT AND DELAYED DAYS

In our recounting, we're going to whiz quickly through the rest of Moses' story. His mother hides him, his sister, Miriam, works the plan to save him, the daughter of Pharaoh raises him, but God pricks Moses' heart for *his true people*, the Israelites. He sees an Israelite being beaten, murders the Egyptian who is beating the Israelite, and then flees to a place called Midian out of fear and shame. Moses stays in Midian, where he marries a woman named Zipporah and where he is seemingly happy pretending as though his people aren't still massively suffering under the oppression of Pharaoh. Who doesn't forget? God. And He comes to Moses with a proposition.

Exodus 3 may be one of my all-time favorite passages in the Bible, but possibly not for reasons you'd think. When most people think of God calling Moses into ministry, they think about him taking off his shoes because it's holy ground or they think about the burning bush. Maybe they picture God's booming voice saying, "I Am Who I Am." That's all incredible, especially when we read this as a historical document and not just as some allegory that tells us something about ourselves. When we blink and shake our heads and remember there was an actual man named Moses who was literally hiding from his past and shirking his present, and God came to him through a bush that was straight-up on fire and an audible voice from heaven—that's some crazy stuff.

Moses and God go on to have some more hard-to-picture-for-us moments, but there's one thing about this initial interaction that I can never get over.

Here's a crazy-quick recap of Exodus 3 and 4, the extreme CliffsNotes version. Moses has run from his problems in the biggest way—he's tending flocks in the wilderness, seemingly trying to squash the memory of his people's burdens. Suddenly, an angel of the Lord calls to Him, and God speaks to him through flames of fire inside a bush. Moses' interest is piqued, and he moves closer to see what's up.

Here's what I catch: God is constantly telling Moses WHAT *He* is going to do and WHO *He* is, and Moses is constantly questioning how *Moses* will do it and who God has made *Moses* to be.

If the questions we're left with after hearing that we're the girls for the job, that we're the rescue plan, have anything to do with *why us* or *how we'll do it*, the story of Moses tells us right off the bat that we're asking the wrong questions.

The answer to "Why me?" is this: *God is who He says He is.*

The answer to "How could you use me?" is this: *He'll be the one doing the heavy lifting.*

I can unequivocally declare that you're the girl for the job, without knowing you or your circumstances, because I know God. Because I know He's all-powerful, all-knowing, always loving. I know He wouldn't leave you behind or fail to give you what you need. Because He's the author and finisher of our faith, and the writer of every human story, I know He's working it all out for us to experience as much of Him as we can—for us to see His glory. Because He's good and because He's a restorer, I know that no harm that has come your way and no bad decision you've made has the power to define you. I know that you're the girl for the job because He's God, and He placed you where you're at, on purpose, to bring Him glory and change the world.

The thing is, *I don't want you to miss it. I don't want us to miss it.*

God is not going to stop showing up or walk away from us. He's not going to give up on His master plan to use human beings to bring Him glory, no matter how messed up we are. I know He is not surprised by your unique set of challenges: the things that keep you from living the abundant life He crafted for you. *But I do believe we have the opportunity to stay behind.* In His graciousness, He's given us the capacity to choose how we respond to Him, and if we're not giving God our 100 percent yes, we may miss how He has ordained our particular role in the rescue.

Moses questioned God's decision to use him over and over, and God got tired of Moses telling Him he didn't have what it takes, but God still gave Moses a helper: his brother, Aaron. God provided miracle after miracle to prove His power, not just to Pharaoh, but also to bolster the faith of Moses—and still Moses doubted and questioned God. He questioned His provision, His protection, and His ability to show up. And throughout the tumultuous years of his leadership, while Moses was appointed pastor to these Israelites, God provided miraculously, and still they struggled with doubt.

God kept using Moses—his doubt didn't disqualify him, but there were consequences when Moses confused whose capacity would do the heavy lifting. Moses often struggled to understand that God was the hero of this whole plan, and it eventually cost him.

God still had Moses lead the people. He still had incredible and awe-inspiring encounters with Moses, letting him see parts of Himself no other human had seen. But when it came time to enter the land and take hold of what God had promised for them, God allowed another leader to take charge. What should have been an eleven-day journey from Egypt to the land appointed for the Israelites took forty years, thanks to their fear, grumbling, and lack of trust in the God who had physically and supernaturally rescued them. And Moses, the man God had handpicked to lead them, died just before they crossed the border. God warned him he wouldn't see the end of this road before dying, and Moses didn't fight Him. I wonder if Moses relented because, in hindsight, he could see the severity of his doubt in God's power and ability. Even though he knew he was wildly special to God, did Moses also feel regret over the moments when he could have trusted Him more? God Himself buried Moses, the Israelites mourned for thirty days, and then their new leader helped them take their promised-by-God land.

WE ARE THE VARIABLE

We've got work to do, friends. Our world is hurting, our church is suffering, our generations are helpless and harassed and in need of a Savior. God, our Father and Friend, has placed you in this exact slice of time, arranging every relationship, circumstance, strength, weakness, and gift in your life to uniquely equip you to shine His light and build His kingdom. But we have to settle something here and now, before we start looking at the tools He's placed in our hands.

We have to take ourselves out of the running. We've got to give up on the pursuit of being the best or even doing it *right*, because it's His power and His purpose that were always meant to do the heavy lifting. We've got to leave behind this picture of our ideal selves that we hoped we'd eventually become; we've got to quit hiding who we are, so we don't get hurt or hurt anyone else. And in the name of Jesus, we've got to quit telling God He's got the wrong girl because (A) if we don't acknowledge that He knows better by this point in the game, we're being crazy, and (B) eventually He may listen to us and use someone else. And then we'll be the ones missing out.

Let's settle this in our hearts before we move forward:

God is God. God is the Hero. We are blessed to be a part of His rescue plan.

God is God, but we are the gals He's ordained to bring light and life to the corner of the world where He has intentionally placed us for mission.

If we believe He is on the throne, then we can trust what He says about us: *We are the girls for the job.*

Let no one say otherwise. Not even ourselves.

FIND YOUR PEOPLE

What if finding your people is less about being comfortable and more about becoming who God created you to be?

CHAPTER 4

LET'S REDEFINE THE STARTING LINE

I got my first F in fifth grade, in English, hilariously. And if that doesn't straight-up disqualify me from being an author of Christian women's books, here's the next doozy. I got my first F in fifth grade, and I deviously plotted and practiced until I could use a dull graphite pencil skillfully enough to make the F look like it was a B on the thin, pink sheet of carbon copy paper so my parents wouldn't know.

The same year I got the infamous F, I also won a writing award at my school, leading me to believe young Jess had the most serious case of not applying herself that anyone may have ever seen. I loved, loved, loved to read and write but hated to do homework. Words were a ticket to expression and stories were a passage to other places, but assignments and due dates were like shackles that kept me bound. And I, apparently, refused to be contained.

My early defeat in literary learning only continued to take root and blossom in college. While I'd barely made it through high school because I was so allergic to applying myself, I somehow miraculously got into college. The only thing that even slightly sparked my interest educationally was writing and reading, so I headed toward an English degree.

Do you know how much you have to read and write to get an English degree? I like to do those things for enjoyment, not as a form of punishment or self-chastisement. But English majors of the world, I applaud you! You read and wrote so much. I did not. I dropped the English major like a bad habit the first month of college.

What I'm trying to tell you is that for these two reasons, and a million others, no one would have expected me to write books. My point? *The starting line isn't where you think it is.*

LET'S CALL HER SARAH

The starting line for me as an author certainly wasn't my incredible grades in school, but it *was* in college—specifically, with a new friend. My freshman year, the same year I realized an English degree would not work out for me, God set a fire in my heart that would ultimately consume me in the best ways.

I'll be the first to admit I went to college with atypical motivations. It was a miracle that I got accepted in the first place, so we can rule out showing off my educational prowess as one of the reasons I was eager to attend a four-year university. I'd already gone through a pretty dark phase of rebellion in high school, before I started walking with Jesus, so it wasn't the parties I was interested in. I didn't crave autonomy or independence, and I was already dating the boy I planned to marry, so I wasn't looking for a soulmate. But I had heard wondrous, glorious things about the campus ministries and Christian community at my particular school.

FCA. Baptist Collegiate Ministry. Worship nights. Local churches' college ministries. My sister had attended the same school just three years ahead of me and found a wealth of community: Christian friends to connect with, places to serve and lead, and a handful of Jesus-centered events to pick from every week. What high schooler picks a college for its Christian community? The kind who is going to be a ministry-church-people-of-God junkie for the rest of her life. I absolutely should have seen the foreshadowing.

The day we moved into the freshman dorms, as my parents hauled boxes up and down seven flights in the sticky South Carolina heat, I excitedly ran from room to room, surveying the situation and trying to figure out the one burning question at the forefront of my mind: *Where are all the Christians?*

I squealed inwardly as I noticed one gal writing a Bible verse on the tiny mirror that came standard with our dorm rooms. "Oh!" I said, "I see you like the Bible! Me too! I love this verse! Do you want to go to church while you're here? I hear there's a big church offering free lunch for college students tomorrow—do you want to go with me?"

The next morning—you know, the first morning of college, when thousands of young adults have been suddenly freed from the bondage of their parents' boundaries and borders and were incredibly likely to sleep in—I was up early. I'd convinced eight women from my floor to go to church with me, even though my car only held five, so we were stuffed in like sardines in the salty, southeastern heat as we drove to church. It was all happening; my dreams were coming true.

We had a great morning, but a week later the newness had begun to wear off, classes had begun, and sororities had started recruiting—and my little girl gang was dwindling and growing all at once. There were still one or two women on my actual floor who were interested in the same things I was, but I was meeting other friends on different floors and in different buildings who'd come to college looking for the same vibrant Christian community I had. Or even if they hadn't come looking, they were taking steps toward it now.

But I couldn't move on so quickly—my heart was attached to these gals I'd first met and grown to love, particularly to the one with the Scripture written on her mirror, the one who'd gone to church with me once and never come back. The one whose personality seemed to change suddenly, when the parties started happening. Let's call her Sarah.

Like I said, I'd already sown my wild oats, done my fair share of drinking and drugs, and had a handful of promiscuous encounters before I met Jesus. So it wasn't Sarah's drinking and the partying that concerned me. In the close quarters of the dorm, sharing bathroom sinks and seeing each other before meals and at the end of the day, I saw an exhaustion settle over her—a thick, dark cloud seemed to roll in and settle. Her eyes looked weary, she started losing weight rapidly, and all the sparkle and sweetness seemed to have been leached from her face as reality settled in: she was looking for her identity, purpose, and approval around every corner of this new-to-us campus. I began to worry it might just do her in.

As we'd brush our teeth in the morning, I'd smell the alcohol still seeping out of her pores. As we'd walk to class, she'd tell me about the boys she'd been with the night before. Sarah would try to make light of their casual post-coital dismissal of her; she'd try to act like it was par for the course, but I worried there was more going on. She seemed like a girl who was getting her heart handed to her every single morning, drinking at night to escape the pain of rejection and the reality that she wasn't sure who she was anymore. Then she'd do it all over again in a cycle that often gets branded as normal collegiate self-discovery, but which was really just self-destruction. I watched and listened and prayed as I saw my newfound friend changing before my eyes. I had a feeling this wasn't normal freshman-year experimentation, this was a girl on the brink of serious pain.

One Thursday night, I was running late for some Christian community event when someone knocked on my door. It was a friend of Sarah's, a gal I'd never met, and she asked me if I'd come to Sarah's room. Sarah had consumed too much alcohol that night and needed a babysitter, the girl said, just in case things got hairy.

For the next few hours, I sat by Sarah's bedside debating whether I should call an ambulance. Was this alcohol poisoning? Was she still breathing? Honestly, I could barely tell. She was still and pale; the only sign of life was a harrowing moan she'd let out every hour or so. IPhones weren't a thing yet, Google wasn't even a thing among college students yet, so I couldn't just quickly research the signs without leaving her side. I sat beside her praying, talking to God—asking Him why he'd placed me on this floor. Why had He let me see her writing that Bible verse on her mirror on move-in day? I was broken for her.

In the morning, when she was awake (and incredibly ill), her friends chided me for my concern and acted like I was an idiot for caring so much. Sarah couldn't meet my gaze, either because of shame or the sick, hungover fog that kept her from really opening them.

That morning, after Sarah's long night of sickness, I made a decision. In all the praying, pondering, and listening to God about why I found myself living in that particular hall of freshman girls, why I had been tagged to nurse a drunk girl, why He'd made me to care so much about their souls and identities and purposes, I'd come up with a plan. I was choosing to believe He'd placed me there on purpose, for our collective good and His glory. I was choosing to believe He wanted me to love them and tell them about Jesus with everything I had. I resolved to show up with my actions, nursing them back to health on nights when they drank too much or making Diet Coke runs when people got low. But I also resolved to use my words.

That afternoon I took a sheet of paper and a pen, knocked on the door of each room, and asked the gals to write down their email addresses. Now, in 2019, authors would call this "list-building"—gathering email addresses so you can send people words to their inboxes. But in 2002, you might have just called it "the annoying girl in the freshman dorm who demands email addresses." Most of them forked over their college email handles, and I told them they could expect some daily devotionals coming their way.

Had I ever written a devotional at this point? No. Did I have any formal Bible teaching? No way. Did I probably say some absolutely crazy things? You'd better believe it. But throughout that year, I just wrote little, daily Bible messages—glimpses of grace, hope, love, and abundance—and I sent them to the emails of the ladies who lived on the seventh floor of my freshman dorm, whether they liked it or not.

Did anyone ask me or invite me? Only Jesus. What qualification did I have? Ambassador of Christ. Was my email campaign met with wild reviews, did it go viral, did one million people know about it? No. Did I ever hear or see proof that it helped a single gal? To be honest, no.

But it was a start. I was burdened for these young women who seemed to be so harassed and helpless, who were struggling with the same things I had struggled with myself or was still struggling with. And it helped me process my concern—writing was a safe way to show them I cared. It was a start that was all about love, that was premeditated with an obsession to see my sister-friends live the abundant life they were created for.

The starting line isn't where you think it is. When we picture the initial steps of obedience—saying yes to Jesus or stepping forward in faith—let's not picture shiny moments or big accomplishments. The starting lines that lead to personal triumphs are not always the starting lines that lead to God's glory. But when we're rooted in a desire to serve, help, and love others well, we'll be set up for mission in a beautiful way.

IT'S NOT ENOUGH

In my coaching and mentoring work, I see so much confusion among women about starting out in their various ministries. I'm not a certified life coach, and I certainly never felt qualified to tell grown women what they should do or how they should do it, but I noticed that as God grew my platform to write, teach, and lead online, women wanted to know how I got started, and they wanted a little guidance on what they should do next.

I've always thought that I shouldn't call it coaching but "mirroring," because often the best thing I can do for a woman is reflect her own words back to her. I ask her to describe why she wants coaching, where she wants to go, and what she is trying to build or grow, and then, for the better part of the session, I ask a lot more questions. What do you mean by that? What would happen if that fear did come true? Why do you care what they think? Who told you it was going to go that way?

The women I meet with mostly hold their own answers; they just need someone to ask the hard questions. I think the same is probably true for you as well, friend. I think about what God has called you to and where He's placed you—in this particular season, but also in the scope of your whole life. I think about what gifts He's given you and what weaknesses He's allowed to remain for your good and His glory. I think about what in the world would have caused you to pick up this book. Are you fed up with the fear and the comparison that's keeping you from being the woman you *know* you were created to be? Are you already in the thick of ministering, and loving and living His dream for your life, but still just dying for someone to tell you that you were meant to do it? Maybe you've been holding back all this time, scared to make your way to the starting line because you're convinced God can't use you, your story, or your gifts.

Let's back up. For the very first time in this book, I'd like to clearly define "the job" that I've so boldly declared I believe you're the girl (Woman! Gal! Lady! Lass!) for.

The "job" is this:

Living the abundant life God has crafted for you with intention, passion, and willingness to do whatever He's asked you to with a fine-tuned focus on His glory.

I believe you were meant to abundantly experience every single day, waking up with the clarity and conviction that God has put you there on purpose to bring light and life and hope to everyone around you. I believe you were called and equipped to change the world, moving it nearer to the kingdom of God and praying that the people around you are called into abundant lives here on earth and eternal lives in heaven. I believe your hands will be most at ease, your heart will be most free, and your mind will be most at peace when you've said yes to the call He's given you. And I believe that you'll only believe it's all worth it when you're doing it for God's glory and the good of others. Whether you ever see the fruit or not, I feel that we *know* by the power of the Holy Spirit when something is done for our glory or His, when it's building His kingdom or ours. I don't think you were made to draw in the sand of these earthly days, your accomplishments and stories washed away with the next generation. I think God has handcrafted you and sent you to use what you've got to make a mark in how eternity is played out—even in the midst of mundane days, tough seasons, and moments when the hard realities of life shake us to our core.

I think you're the girl for the job, but the starting line for this real and beautiful kingdom race is probably not where you think it is. If the beginning of our mission is rooted in our dreams, our giftedness, our desire for fame or notoriety, or anything that rests on our capacity, desires, tenacity, or glory, we're done for. It just won't be enough. None of those things will ever power us through, and any desire we have to see them come to fruition will be dashed when life inevitably happens, and we prove ourselves human.

Our dreams and visions for our life, for what we're supposed to do and what we're hoping for, are *powerful*. I'm a believer in the powerful process of partnering with the Holy Spirit to cast vision, to see visions, to dream about what could be. But when our dreams are exposed to reality, they can lose a lot of the power and weight they once carried. If our hope is in the dream, it's a shallow and fleeting one that we can't quite stand firm on.

As you hopefully heard in my story, I had the distinct luxury of not being able to start from a place of giftedness since I had such a low-achieving beginning to life, but honestly, I think *our* ability is an incredibly dangerous footing to build a life on, a ministry on, because it elevates us from the beginning and always sets us up to fail. Someone is smarter than you, stronger than you, wiser than you. Someone can sing better, mother better, lead better. Someone is tougher and more tender. Someone has had the advantage of more training or was born more naturally gifted.

When we build on our own gifts and strengths, we'll be dismayed by the strength of others and never start, or we'll quit early when we ultimately don't live up to our potential, make a misstep, or inevitably fail to execute on our aptitude.

For so many of us who have excited and encouraged ourselves by manifesting the power of our own visions and dreams or who have taken stock of our strengths and held them at the starting line like trophies we earned, this can feel disheartening. I can picture a horde of women in our generation holding their figurative gifts with disappointed faces—weary from bolstering our own hearts and from using our dreams to pump ourselves up for the fight—wondering where we go from here.

Hold on to those dreams and those gifts; don't cast them

aside just yet. God has given them to you to use as weapons of mass destruction against the forces of darkness you're going to fight for His glory. But they're *tools* you can use, not ground you're going to want to stand on. And let's not be disheartened by that, because the starting line may not be where we thought it was, but it's somewhere so much better.

If we're going to make a lasting impact, if we're going to go for the long haul, if we're to partner with God to build eternity brick by brick, day by day, for the glory of God, *the starting line is His capacity and His character*. The terra firma beneath our feet will be His promises and His purposes for our lives; we won't have to fight to find them or look further than where He's placed us. And the room we've been given to run the path marked out for us isn't limited by our lack of ability but made and intentionally productive by His enduring capacity.

Simply put, if we lean our full weight on Him, we'll go as far as He can go, and we'll fight as hard as He can fight. We will love as He loves. We won't be limited by our humanity but powered by His supernatural Spirit. The prize we win at the end will not be the celebration of our accomplishments, but the indescribable beauty of His glory on display and the life-giving and life-changing knowledge that we gave all that we had so He could be praised and His goodness could be displayed.

The starting line might not be where you think it is, because we don't get to draw it. And this is good news, because the pressure's off! It's not about our capacity; it has always been about God's. So we can stop second-guessing ourselves and lean our full weight on the capacity of the One who calls us.

CHAPTER 5

WHO ARE YOU BROKEN FOR?

"How did you get into ministry? Did you always dream of being a pastor or leader?"

"Nope—I actually committed murder, and it was all up from there."

Let's dig back into Moses' story, because it's quite a story. When we left him a few chapters ago, we were just starting to get acquainted with his life, looking over the broad strokes of his timeline, the arc of his ministry, and how God would use his leadership to get the Israelites out of slavery and into the land he had promised them.

Now that we've quit our pursuit of being the best, taken ourselves out of the running for any and all accolades, and recognized that the starting line is rarely where we think it is, let's see how Moses comes back around to confirm all these truths.

I can still remember the first time I read through Exodus and Deuteronomy. I got to the end of Moses' life and thought, *Man, what a goof.* You want to talk about starting lines for ministry? Murder was Moses' starting line!

"So how did God commission you and call you to the specific and beautiful plan for how He wanted to use you? Was it at a worship service? Did you have a dream? Did the pastor you grew up with send you a letter speaking into all the amazing gifts God had given you?"

"Um, no. I killed a guy and ran for my life, then saw a bush that didn't burn up and heard God speaking audibly through it."

"Oh! A burning bush! An encounter with the One True God! Tell me more!"

"Well, I argued with Him. A lot. He kept telling me how He was going to use me, and I continually debated with Him (because I was self-conscious about my stutter) until He finally got annoyed enough to agree to let my brother help me out."

Kind of a goofball starting line, to say the least, right? But Moses went on to lead the Israelites—to partner with God on behalf of His people, to serve and lead and give all that He had to shepherding them. But man, that start was not shiny or cute. *And then it got even worse.*

One day, after Moses had grown up, he went out to where his own people were and watched them at their hard labor. He saw an Egyptian beating a Hebrew, one of his own people. Looking this way and that and seeing no one, he killed the Egyptian and hid him in the sand. (Exodus 2:11–12)

Murder. Those words we just read, let's put a little flesh on them. Moses had committed an act of rage that couldn't be undone—taking another human's life. Moses was a murderer.

It's mostly accepted that Moses wrote these chapters of the Bible, but there's also room for other possibilities. If it *was* Moses, he gets a lot more credit in my book for including his absolute worst moments and not painting himself in a more favorable light. He wrote about the murder, about arguing with God over his stutter, and about all the blunders he made along the way, even about claiming the power of God as his own! I'm grateful the Bible was directed by the power of the Holy Spirit, and I can only imagine the supernatural intervention God our Father might have used as Moses wrote these scrolls, retelling so many of his own stories. Maybe an angel stood over him and said, "Bro! *Do not leave out the murder part.*" I get that in a small way, as often when I'm writing, the Holy Spirit will prick my heart and show me how I'm describing myself in a much better light than I should.

Anyhow, I'm glad this part is brief, but I'd still like to see the cinematic historical replay when I get to heaven. How long did Moses stand there watching the beating? How long had he known he wasn't an Egyptian, but an Israelite? Since childhood? Did he find it out dramatically? We're not told; we skip straight from his rescue as an infant to this powerful reckoning moment when his burden explodes into action.

Here's the thing: obviously, Moses' vengeance-inspired homicide, stealthy cover-up, and subsequent run-for-the-hills is not a shining example of faith. But I *do* think we get a glimpse into what kept Moses ministering to the Israelites for forty years in a literal and figurative desert.

He was broken for his people. So broken that his burden bubbled over into rage. He couldn't *not* act on behalf of his people any longer. Later, the sovereignty of God and the holiness of the Most High would be the beckoning point that kept him faithful, but the very first moments of Moses' leadership revolved around *His people.*

What we do *not* see is Moses sitting in his room in the palace, dreaming about how *he* must be destined for something great. What we do *not* see is Moses counting his strengths as he watches other leaders, strategizing how he can use what he's got to build something beautiful or unite a nation. If any of those things had been the starting line for Moses, he could have stayed in Egypt and used the man-made power that had been handed to him. Instead, his leadership was rooted in a burden for others and a belief in the sovereignty of God.

We should beware of anyone on mission, including ourselves, who speaks more of what they've been made for or what they want to build and less of the people for whom they're burdened. We should pause and pray when the conversations in our lives revolve more around our giftings and less around the groaning in our hearts for those God has given us to lead. We should learn from Moses, not necessarily from his actions, but most definitely from his passion—brokenness for others is the most beautiful starting line we can ever have for ministry.

We can also learn from what we *don't* see in Moses' story—we don't see him taking advantage of the affluent leadership that would have been offered to him inside Pharaoh's house. The world will tell us we should plant ourselves in the most favored-looking place, where we can have the greatest worldly impact and see the most fruit of our labors. But God's kingdom doesn't abide by the rules and workings of the world. Instead, it often calls us to start broken, burdened, and busted, because it's that yearning for the good of others that will keep us going.

So as we look to God's starting line, and lean into God's capacity, ask yourself: What are you broken for? Who are you broken for? And let's also take a good, hard look at the brokenness within ourselves to see what He has to work with.

We can start by repenting of any and all selfish ambition we've harbored, asking God to give us an earnest desire for His glory instead. We can start by asking what He has planned— what *He* would like us to do. We can keep His capacity and compassion (both of which are boundless) in clear view, taking our hands off the plan and refusing to assign our human limits to His potential vision for our lives.

And then, we can start with people. We can open our eyes to see the pain of those around us and allow ourselves to be broken with them and for them. We can allow ourselves to be consumed with a passion to use what we've got to bring them closer to God's best for them. Whether our people are in the palace or the poorhouse, we just need to open our eyes and ask our Father to help us see them how He does.

LET'S FLIP THE SCRIPT

I want to pause and acknowledge now that where we're headed in the next few moments may sound pretty countercultural. I would blame Taylor Swift, but it's not really her fault. In recent years, the idea of growing your squad, your tribe, your girl gang, your crew has become increasingly popular. It seems that women all over the world are expected to have a group of gals they belong to. These are our friends, but more than that, they're a huge representation of who we are and what we belong to.

I really don't think this was TSwift's idea, because we don't need to go further than the Word of God to see beautiful, vibrant descriptions of community. We're created in the image of God, our triune God who literally operates seamlessly in community: the Father, His Son, and the Holy Spirit. So our desire to want to belong to a people, to a group, to a crew is good and right.

But as we're talking specifically about the people we're called to love and serve, I think it might be wise to pop the hood and see what's happening in our relationships. Are they leading us to give God more glory? Are they spurring us on to pursue the good of the world around us?

Again, I'm a community girl, a friend girl, and there is nothing I love more than going on a run with a few girlfriends or grabbing coffee and catching up on our lives. I love my friends. I love having women with whom I can talk about life! But this wonderful gift of community and belonging can take a quick downturn when we begin to make too much of our tribe, over and above the mission to which God has called us.

I'm going to put some real words here, words I've shared a handful of times with other women, only to watch them tear up and nod slowly in affirmation. I've found that women often fall into two groups:

a. Some women feel left out of the tribe mentality altogether, like they missed that lesson in elementary school. I had one friend cry to me a few years ago because no one ever taught her how to use foundation or host a great slumber party. I remember telling her: *Me either*. I don't think those lessons ever took place.

b. I've found that there is a host of women who do have a crew of tight-knit friends, but *they still feel alone*, and maybe even anxious that their tribe keeps them from thriving and living their most abundant life.

Could it be that our hopes are not aimed correctly when we're picturing these groups of gals to run with? Could it be that maybe the *picture* of what is "healthy" is off, not an entire generation of women? Let's look at a picture of what could be, in the best-case scenario, before we dig in any further.

Let's start with Jesus, who was literally perfect and could have picked anyone in the whole world to be his ride-or-die folks, but who picked twelve ordinary guys. Let's back up even more and look at the Urban Dictionary definition of "ride or die," as it's a common phrase used in conjunction with words like tribe, squad, girlfriend, and so on.

"Ride or die" was originally a biker term meaning if you couldn't ride, you'd rather die. It has now changed to mean anyone (wife, boyfriend, best friend) with whom you will wiliingly "ride" out a problem or "die" trying. The "ride" doesn't always have to be negative, either. Obviously if you're this close to someone, you want them to enjoy the "ride" (life and all it has to offer with them as well).

So if we're looking at Jesus and His crew, or His squad, I'd say for sure He was willing to ride out any problems or die trying to love them, but the reciprocation wasn't always there, right? Peter denied Him, John was constantly trying to prove Jesus loved Him the most, and Judas completely betrayed Him. All of them missed the signs He gave them regarding what was to come, and after He was dead, they went into hiding. Of the twelve who walked with Him, learned from Him, and had the most exposure to Him, only John was present at His death.

I'd say *He* was their ride or die, but not even Jesus experienced a squad or a tribe who had His back in the most important moment of His earthly life. Still, He chose them intentionally, with full knowledge of who they were and how they would treat Him. So I surmise this about Jesus: He may not have picked the people who made Him feel the best, who cheered Him on the greatest, but He surrounded Himself with those who would help Him bring the most glory to God.

Scripture doesn't necessarily preach an ideology of finding your tribe for the sake of your comfort. Instead, when it comes to friendships, relationships, and groups of community in the Word of God, we hear a call to give ourselves away. We hear a call to grace, which means that we have full sight of one another's sins and yet we are still pointing to truth. The Bible paints a picture of messy, beautiful relationships that are based not on how we make each other feel but instead focused on how the world is impacted when we come together.

The last point I'll share (I have many more, but we don't have time to cover them all) is that the idea of tribes and squads isn't necessarily biblical *or* gracious, because they have the potential to become exclusive and harmful to those outside the tribe. We do see Jesus drawing away with different groups of disciples for intimacy's sake—He'd pull away with the twelve, or even just three on occasion. And I agree that a small group of individuals sharing intimate moments and growth is wildly beautiful. But where we've taken it, in current culture, especially our internet culture, there is an inherent danger that one's "tribe" can unintentionally perpetuate the feeling that everyone else is on the outside and failing to do community successfully. The "tribe" can incite unhealthy comparisons, feelings of jealousy and/or bitterness, and other negative responses if we don't take the utmost care.

Rather than our intimate moments in relationships embodying clarity, growth, and grace that spur us on to good works outside of our small tribes, it seems we're building higher walls and greater barriers that discourage anyone else who might want to be included. It seems as though we, as a culture, collect friendships and social groups like medals or badges of honor, proclaiming how great we are to have these people, to be one of them, to *belong*. We've forgotten we belong to the family of God first and foremost, and that affiliation has lost its weight as we've longed to fit in with a crew here on earth.

If you have an incredible group of women with whom you spend your days, I want you to know I'm not coming after your squad here. I'm not encouraging you to break up the band or dismantle the years of intimacy and encouragement you've built. But this is an invitation to look over your shoulder and perhaps open your eyes to the other people surrounding you. Does your tribe spur others on to intimacy with God and the rest of the kingdom or is it just hurtful to others to be excluded? Is your tribe growing in grace and truth—are you challenging each other with ideas and questions that fall outside your comfort zones? Are you missing out on the different colors, flavors, or spices of humanity that others in your community have to offer? And are you open to others joining you, to extending hospitality and inclusivity, or is your circle closed?

If you'll bear with me, I've got a few more questions about your friend group. Do you think there is any potential you may be missing out on seeing people to whom God has called you to minister because the maintenance of your squad takes all your time, energy, service, tears, celebration, and burden? Could it be that you don't have much left over to give the world around you because only your tribe is getting your best?

Finally, could it be that sometimes the bulk of your relational energy goes to "your people" and you wonder why you struggle to feel intimate with God? If your first instinct is to call them, confess to them, celebrate with them, run your ideas by them, vent to them, or even just fill your moments of margin with their presence, is your soul growing more accustomed to the noise and vibes of the tribe rather than the quietness and depth of time with God?

Here's the thing: these are tough questions. I'm grateful you're still with me here, and I want you to know these are questions I've struggled with myself. Sometimes the answers have been hard to bear, and sometimes the Holy Spirit has comforted me with the truth that my friendships are, in fact, growing the kingdom and spurring others on to new life.

For those of you without a tribe, you don't have to ask these hard questions. If this is you, I want to acknowledge for a moment that I'm with you, sister. I'm at the tail end of repenting from a season wherein I wanted to belong more than I wanted to be used by God. I wanted to be liked and approved of by the women in my community more than I wanted to be connected to those who could best help me move the kingdom of God forward. Somewhere in the back of my mind, I was convinced I could win over these women whose approval I coveted and gain their affection, and I pined for it like an adolescent schoolgirl. You can probably guess that the harder I tried, the more I was rejected, and I'm left now with a year of hurtful memories from a crew of women in my community who decided I was not their cup of tea.

What I understand now is that God was protecting me from belonging here on earth so I could see other women with kingdom eyes. He was providing manna in relationships, in pockets of people or time wherein He would fill up my heart, and I absolutely believe that can be true for you, too. I believe that His presence is more powerful and pervasive than that of any girl squad. I think His friendship is purer and more uplifting. And I know that I know that belonging in heaven will trump belonging to people on earth any day of the week.

Throughout the rest of this book, I'm offering a new way to view "our people." I pray it will be equally useful to those of you who have a million best friends and to those of you who feel very alone. If our job is to use what we've got, for the good of others and the glory of God, we need core people in our lives we can walk with and be encouraged by. But let's also widen the circle and practice being present to the people around us—the people God may be giving us opportunities to bless, encourage, enrich, and serve.

WHO ARE MY PEOPLE?

Some of you already know who your people are. My daughter, Glory, has had a people she feels calls to minister to almost longer than she's had a relationship with Jesus. When she was as young as four or five, she began waving at homeless people. That sounds sweet and kind and human, but her waving was so extra and precious, I can barely describe it.

Let's say there's a soul slumped over in a doorway in the middle of a big city, with hundreds and even thousands of people passing them every hour. Some people might drop some change in a cup for them and some might hand them a meal they'd purchased, but most would ignore them, and a handful wouldn't even realize they were there. Glory, on the other hand, will wave at them until they catch her eye, stooping into their field of vision and making sure they see her saying hello. She wants people without a home to know she sees them and loves them.

When she was seven, she started enlisting our help to make peanut butter and jelly sandwiches to hand out to the homeless. I buy the supplies and oversee the process, but for the most part, she runs the show. She usually prefers that I sit in the car and watch as she hands out meals to her friends. She's never scared—these are her people.

I was never more certain that the homeless were the people who would tug at Glory's heartstrings than when we rode the subway the first time our family visited New York City. Passion, action, and compassion are great indicators of calling, but also your emotions—in particular, a sense of being overwhelmed—are an indicator as well. As we rode the subway, occasionally surrounded by people who carried their belongings in trash bags or were asking for money, sometimes my compassionate girl would become overwhelmed by empathy, unable to summon the needed strength to face the pain of others. And right there on the subway, she'd curl up on the seat, pull her legs into her jacket, bury her head between her knees, close her eyes, and cover her ears.

It wasn't a desire to stop seeing people in need or a lack of love that led her to withdraw—it was that she cared so much and the need was too great, and she needed to draw into herself for some quiet so she could keep going.

Now, let's pause. Some of you are perhaps tearing up in empathy because you have felt this way about a people group, maybe even the same people group as my Glory. But I've got a strong feeling that there is also a large crew of you who are feeling ashamed or fearful because you don't feel this way about people who are living on the streets, and what's even more terrifying is that you're not sure you've ever felt this broken or burdened for anyone else.

That doesn't make you a sociopath, okay? Stay with me, here.

Remember how we've already quit and taken ourselves out of the running? I'm not in line to try to be the most compassionate or the most mission-minded. Jesus already won that award when He went to the cross to die for the sins of the whole world. So when I see that my own daughter, who I am supposed to be *leading*, is more stirred to action for a people group than I am, I've got an opportunity.

The way I see it, we have a choice:

1. We can feel threatened, insecure, and even angry. Because someone else has a heart for a people and we don't, we can discount that passion and make up reasons why that person shouldn't help those people she cares about. We can pretend as though we already do help them, which is prideful lying. We can quietly and coldly suggest "more helpful" or needier groups of people she could be ministering to, pulling her into the shame circle and robbing her of the joy of serving those God has put on her heart to serve. We can even take on the burden God has given her, pretending to come alongside her, even though it may be ill-fitting for us, leaving us exhausted and unsure of what we're called to in the first place.

or . . .

2. We can feel thankful that the Holy Spirit speaks to her. We can actually feel bolstered and encouraged in our faith to know that He communicates differently with each of us, and that can even further convince us of His power, grace, and holiness. We can learn from her, taking tips from what she does, without taking on the whole burden He's given her to carry.

Sister, if you already know the people group God has put on your heart to minister to in this season, *praise Him*. Maybe you're burdened for women who feel crushed by society's expectations or those who have experienced significant loss. Perhaps you've got single women on your heart or you've got a message of hope for recovering perfectionists. Maybe it's some people group I can't even imagine. Whatever it is, I praise Him *for* you. If He's put blond Christian authors in their early thirties on your heart to minister to, holler at your girl and I'll tell you my shoe size and address. *Just making sure you're paying attention.*

If He's already zoomed in on a people group for you, great! But please don't make the mistake of believing it needs to be the same people group for everyone around you. God has given *you* that burden so you can help carry it by His grace and through His power, but if you begin to shame others for not caring about the same thing, you may place yokes on them they were not created to bear.

And if He hasn't shown you yet, if you couldn't guess for a million dollars who He's placed in front of you to love, lead, and bring into the light, then I've got a few questions to help you think through it. But please don't worry, stress, or strive because we've already let Jesus win the prize of being the most burdened for others and the most willing to act.

Can I pray for us? For you and for me, that God would give us eyes right now, because this is a submission that takes refreshing, and it's one I need to take part in as much as I need to lead it.

Father,

You're the hero. We're your daughters, and we're leaving behind the desire to be good, better, best, as well as the desire to be seen as any of those things. We just want to love your people, and we want to be .

intentional by specifically ministering to those you may have put on our hearts or in our paths.

You know better than we do that the world is spinning so fast, with brokenness abounding. We're here to worship—to use our hands, feet, voices, dollars, days, nights, freedom, and futures to bring people into your kingdom and into awareness of your loving-kindness.

So give us eyes to see, God.

We're on your team, and we're so thankful you—the starter and the finisher of this story—are on ours.

We love you.

Amen.

CHAPTER 6

THESE ARE MY PEOPLE

Here's what we know so far:

1. We're the women of God, and we're here on purpose.
2. Our world is hurting, and while Jesus is the hero, He's made us part of the rescue plan.
3. But to join Him, we've first got to quit. We're called to give up on being the hero and take ourselves out of the running to be the best.
4. What's left behind is a desire for His glory and for the good of those He's called us to love and serve. They are our starting line, but who are they? How do we connect with them? How do we know where to find them? This is one of my favorite things to help women figure out—will you jump in with me as we work through this together?

Imagine us now in my office in downtown Charleston, where I do my all-day coaching calls. The walls are the whitest white and hung with brightly colored art. The table is actually a ginormous old desk Nick and I inherited from a ministry in

Seattle, but it's been carried from city to city and painted color after color. Currently it's white, and we've got these amazing high-backed wicker chairs that complement it so well, making you feel like you're sitting at a king's table rather than at a desk where you're about to get some work done.

Placed in front of you is coffee, tea, or LaCroix—whatever you fancy. Your hands are free, so you can gesture wildly or wring them nervously or fidget in your seat. There are no rules. I'm not sitting with you, however, because I'm taking notes on the whiteboard. During one of these all-day, in-person coaching sessions, I scribble notes on the whiteboard so you can see what you're saying, and we ask an assistant to take notes on a laptop, too, so that not one word that slips from your mouth goes missing.

You're wearing whatever makes you feel most comfortable and alive, the clothes that make you feel the most like you. I'm wearing what I call my power dress; it's olive green and super flowy, with buttons from the top to the bottom, and I always wear it with my denim jacket. By this point in the day, my hair is definitely up because we are about to get down to business. *This is where it gets good, friend.*

Maybe I've already asked you who you feel burdened for, and you didn't quite have an answer, or maybe you did have an answer but still want to go through the list of questions to be sure we're on the same track. Either way, I'm excited to hear, and my dry erase marker is poised for action. Let's go.

Who is already listening to you?

Who is already listening to you?

Don't you dare say nobody. Because the truth is that you

interact with people every single day who are paying attention to your every move, learning from what you do and say, and they are undoubtedly impacted by *you*.

They might be your roommate, your parents, your children, your next-door neighbor, your coworkers, your friends, or your boss. They might be many other people as well, but the truth remains the same. As long as people can hear your voice, read your body language, get your emails, or receive your text messages, they're listening to you. You have been empowered to point them to light and life and healing and wholeness just because you have a voice and they are listening.

Here's the number one tip that I find serves women well when it comes to loving those who are already listening to them. Please listen, and let's all tattoo this on our hearts, because it is a game-changer and a mission-maker:

We think our responsibility is to tell everyone how they should interact with Jesus, but what is most life-changing is when we interact with Jesus in front of others and let them see the difference He makes in our lives.

These people who are already listening to you? There may be an occasion where the Holy Spirit asks you to go directly to them with some form of admonishment, correction, or teaching, but it's more likely that what will really impact them the most is seeing Him transform you and hearing you acknowledge that it's Christ doing the work.

Let me give you some examples from my own life. God has allowed me to write books and teach women all over the US about the Word of God, but it's hard for me to imagine there is any greater impact than that I've had on my kids. Because I've taught them so much about the Word? Well, not really.

Because I'm the chief apologizer in our house. I fuss too much? I apologize. I work too hard and don't give them attention; I apologize. They see me get testy with their dad; I apologize. And they see me accept God's grace and move forward, not shamed but spurred on by the mercy with which He's come after me.

Of all the women who might watch what I do online, you know who I tend to pray for the most? The gals with whom I attended high school. A handful of them follow me online, and I see them comment on things occasionally. Maybe they're reading this book. I pray that they will see what I say and do now as a work of God's transforming power and nothing else. Because in high school I was the hottest mess. I didn't just drink like a fish and smoke like a chimney, but I was selfish, insecure, and I struggled with a variety of symptoms that are congruent with mental illness.

My parents, the employees who have been with me for a handful of years, the friends who have loved me through the hard years, and the neighbor who follows me online and also sees me in my bathrobe while I'm letting my dog out every morning before the kids go to school—they see the most authentic, most busted and raw version of me, but they also see the transforming power of Jesus sustaining and upholding me. They see the change in me that comes little by little, and they hear me prayerfully giving glory to God for any and all of the good that comes out this life.

There are people already listening to you, and in the name of Jesus, I believe that you were sent to one another on purpose, for the glory of God, to change the world. The people who are already listening to us are *our* people, like it or not, and a burden for them—a deeply rooted desire for them to take further steps toward abundance—is the best place we can start.

What if they're older than you?

> And don't let anyone put you down because you're young. Teach believers with your life: by word, by demeanor, by love, by faith, by integrity. (1 Timothy 4:12 MSG)

What if they don't love God?

> You are the light of the world. A town built on a hill cannot be hidden. Neither do people light a lamp and put it under a bowl. Instead they put it on its stand, and it gives light to everyone in the house. In the same way, let your light shine before others, that they may see your good deeds and glorify your Father in heaven. (Matthew 5:14–16)

What if they already know God? What do I really have to offer them?

> As iron sharpens iron, so one person sharpens another. (Proverbs 27:17)

> Therefore encourage one another and build each other up, just as in fact you are doing. (1 Thessalonians 5:11)

I could keep going, but the simple fact is this: if you want to change the world, you've got a 100 percent chance to make an impact if you just love the people around you. It's multiplication, it's the ripple effect, and it's how Jesus became a household name. One person tells another person what they know to be true, and they love each other, and it goes on and on.

What if I hurt them or I do it wrong or sin in front of them?

You will! And God will use that!

But he said to me, "My grace is sufficient for you, for my power is made perfect in weakness." Therefore I will boast all the more gladly about my weaknesses, so that Christ's power may rest on me. (2 Corinthians 12:9)

No one is saying you need to love perfectly or serve endlessly the people who are already listening to you. As you apply grace to your own life, they will see the power of the gospel and be impacted. So don't be scared to let them see you sin, stumble, feel weak, worry, or mess up. Jesus is the hero—we already quit trying to be that, right?

Who is already listening to you? *These are some of your people*. Now I want to ask you a few questions to help you continue processing:

1. Have you believed that God's power to use you to encourage and equip those around you has been limited?
2. Who is already listening to you?
3. What do they most need to hear right now?
4. Could you ask God to increase your burden for them, to be propelled by that more than anything else?

BE LIKE JESUS, NOT JONAH

The second group of people we're going to see, hold, and pray for may surprise you, and it may take sorting through some emotions—both good and bad—in order to see them as a beautiful burden rather than a source of frustration.

Let's dive in, fueled by the grace God has given us and powered by the fruit of the Spirit that reminds us we can be loving, patient, gentle, and kind to others because our Father is within us. Ready?

Who makes you angry?

I'll go first on this one, with my palms in the air and all my dirty laundry and secret anger out front for you to see.

In college, I developed an obsession with modesty. It was the early 2000s, and in the Christian world, everyone was a little obsessed with modesty and purity and kissing dating goodbye. My early 2000s Christian gals know what I'm talking about. Looking back, I realize I wasn't really all that obsessed with *purity* or even *modesty*, but with the lack thereof. An obsession with purity and modesty would have made my heart more meek, gentle, and humble—but instead, I was just mad at everyone who seemed, in my opinion, to not be wearing enough clothing.

In those days, I wore a lot of long-sleeved shirts and embarrassingly long and unattractive shorts in the summer, and I looked judgingly at women who chose to wear normal or even slightly revealing clothes. Forget bathing suits. I couldn't reconcile in my mind how it was okay to walk around in what looked like underwear with our brothers in Christ watching, much less talking to them with so much of our bodies exposed.

I got angry, and I got judgy, and after one particularly damaging conversation with another woman, the pastor who supervised me at the church where I was on staff sat me down and corrected me. *I* was the one with the problem, he said, not all these gals. He was right. I was projecting my own issues on them, mainly because I wasn't comfortable in my body, and I needed to get a handle on it.

What I realized as I spent a few months repenting my judgmental attitude and hurtful comments was that there was an actual burden underneath all that shame and blame; I was just handling it and expressing it in a very wrong capacity.

The burden was this: *I wanted women of God to be seen as strong ambassadors for the gospel and not as objectifying tools.*

I was getting hung up on the idea that the clothes a sister in Christ wears may disqualify her from ministry, and in the meantime I was also judging her, deciding for her, and distrusting her ability to hear from the Holy Spirit about what she put on her body.

I repented from that sin, asked God for different eyes with which to see my sisters from then on. I then spent years thinking about the actual burden: *women knowing they are called ambassadors to the King of Kings.*

Fast-forward fifteen years: Do I still care about modesty a lot? *Yes.* Is it the thing I talk about the most or even at all? *No.* Because I know that what I *really* care about is the hearts of the women of God. If they feel judged, classified, or shamed by me, I lose my power to minister to them. If all I'm looking for is behavior modification from them, I lose sight of God's big picture, which is not women made more modest, but women taking their place in His kingdom.

So I'm wondering: Who or what scenario makes you mad? What pricks your pride, your judgment, or your frustration?

Let's quickly contrast the stories of Jonah and Jesus. Maybe you're familiar with both, but it always helps to recap. Jonah was a prophet in the Old Testament who was told by God to go to Nineveh and preach to the people there, calling them to repentance. But Jonah didn't want to go. The Ninevites frustrated him because they were idol worshippers, and he worshipped the one true God. In other words, Jonah didn't feel the Ninevites were deserving of God's grace. He turned his nose up at this city. So he ran from God's call on his life and ended up being swallowed by a huge fish. Finally, he relented and went to preach to the Ninevites. When they heard him, obeyed God, repented, and told God they were sorry, Jonah was still mad, because God forgave them. Jonah did not channel his anger into a passion for his ministry, and because he was so stinking selfish, we're still talking about it today.

Jesus, the Savior and Redeemer of our souls, also knew what it was to burn with a righteous and holy anger. It wasn't all passive preaching on His part; sometimes He used His words to let people know, "This really upsets me, and therefore, this really upsets My Father" (my paraphrase). In Matthew 23, He expresses serious frustration about the Pharisees and hypocrites. In Matthew 16, he refers to Peter, one of His disciples, as "Satan," when Peter tries to separate Him from those He is ministering to. In Mark 11, he flips over tables and yells about the profit-making, business-centric place the temple had become. He raised His voice at demons in an attempt to heal people, and He used His words to cut people to the quick when they were in the wrong. He was full of grace, but also full of truth.

The difference between Jonah and Jesus? *Besides divinity?* Jonah looked down on a city and condemned it. But when Jesus considered a city, He had quite a different response:

When the city came into view, he wept over it. (Luke 19:41 MSG)

Just before the Passover Feast, Jesus knew that the time had come to leave this world to go to the Father. Having loved his dear companions, he continued to love them right to the end . . . So he got up from the supper table, set aside his robe, and put on an apron. Then he poured water into a basin and began to wash the feet of the disciples, drying them with his apron. (John 13:1, 4–5 MSG)

Jesus prayed, "Father, forgive them; they don't know what they're doing." (Luke 23:34 MSG)

I could keep going, filling the rest of this book with passages that show Jesus being compassionate, weeping over His friends, serving people, and giving His life to save them. His anger and frustration were symptoms of His burden, the same burden He carries for you and me today. Jesus desires us to have intimacy with His Father, and He was willing to go to the cross that we might have it. His blood still intercedes on our behalf, making a way for us to walk boldly into the throne room of grace, by the power of the Holy Spirit and for the glory of God and the good of our world.

His anger was real, but it was a symptom of His true burden, and the same can be true for us.

LET'S SEE OTHER PEOPLE

Do you love personality tests? I *love* personality tests. Myers-Briggs, DISC testing, even the one that classifies you as an animal (I'm a lion, by the way). My favorite two are the Enneagram and the Fivefold Ministry Test. I'm an eight on the Enneagram and a Prophet on the Fivefold, and these two things help me feel known and exposed all at once.

But where I think personality tests can do us a small disservice is when we let them pigeonhole us into believing we can't be other things. See, I'm an eight on the Enneagram, but I can also be incredibly loyal, which is the defining characteristic of a six. I can also spend time with ideas and solutions swirling in my head the way a five might, and I can veer toward a strong sense of right and wrong, the way a one does. If I read the description of an eight one time and let myself live into the strength of that description only, I'd become an archetype of a person. And I'm no archetype; I'm a living, breathing, changing, growing gal who is powered by the wind of the Holy Spirit and can move around within my gifts, weaknesses, and strengths.

You are not an archetype, and there isn't just one people group that you are called to see, love, serve, and minister to. Not just one group in this season, and surely not just one season for your whole life. I've made this mistake personally, to the detriment of my own soul and my relationships with others. If I can equip us with anything in this chapter, it will be a prayer to see *people*, all of them, as God sees them, and the discernment to know which people He'd like us to spend time with, which people He'd like us to carry in our hearts.

What's more, it will serve us well to remember that the

people God has called us to love aren't archetypes either. They're whole people with complex stories. They've got strengths and weaknesses just like us; they're not to be put on a pedestal or pitied for their problems. Just as God is mighty in us, He's also mighty *in them*. Wasn't this part of Jonah's issue? He saw himself as better than the people of Nineveh. He saw them as evil instead of possibly on their way to redemption. You are not an archetype; you are not wired to only love one people group, and the people you are called to love are likewise not one-dimensional. This is an active, alive, and colorful story of redemption we're all living here.

In this season of your life, the Father may be asking you to see and love those you interact with on a daily basis, but that doesn't mean you'll only mingle with those people forever. Mamas, He may be asking you to care for the hearts of your children today, but He is not benching you from ministry outside your home forever. You are not an archetype, and your capacity is not solely human; it's endowed with the infinite power of the Creator of the universe. This means you're going to be able to care for varied groups of people over the course of your life, sometimes more than one at a time. In the name of Jesus, I believe that as your capability to love others rises, so will the level of abundance you experience.

The hope is that after we take ourselves out of the running, we will start with a love and a burden for others that increases our understanding of God and how He loves all of us, and that this will spur us to action, to act like the ambassadors of Christ we are. Let's not get tripped up in the *who*, but rather let's be compelled by compassion for *all* the people our Father lets us see, learn from, and love, because He first loved us.

USE WHAT YOU'VE GOT

Your strengths, weaknesses, and story
were written on purpose.

CHAPTER 7

WHAT KIND OF WOMAN

Think back to your Ideal Self—you know, the one we honored for a moment and then gently set aside so we could go on with being our real actual selves? Have you ever thought about how your Ideal Self interacts with God? How she might respond if she met Him? I don't have to think too hard, because I've always had a picture in my head of how Ideal Jess might treat Jesus.

Mary Magdalene, one of the Jewish women who followed Jesus and contributed to His ministry, has always been the embodied form of how Ideal Jess would love to interact with Jesus. Here's a few things we know about my girl MM. Pay close attention here, because a few of these might surprise you.

Mary was from the city of Magdala, a fishing town on the western shore of the Sea of Galilee. First up, I gotta tell you—people put out some straight-up *rumors* about Mary, and in all honesty, I'm currently repenting for any confusion I've caused in the past by not truly understanding who she was. My earliest memories of hearing about Mary Magdalene included being taught that she was a prostitute. While that would illustrate God's grace and compassion to include all kinds of people in his ministry, it's not true. There isn't a clear indication of where the rumor came from, but theologians believe the rumor was started in order to discredit Mary's testimony and the validity of her apostleship. The truth is that she was a woman who followed Jesus, was friends with Jesus, and supported His ministry. Let's put an end to that prostitute rumor.

For most of my Christian life, I also thought Mary Magdalene and Mary, the sister of Martha and Lazarus, were the same person. But nah, that's Mary of Bethany. Totally different, historically real human.

So who *was* Mary Magdalene? Here's what we know about her: She was somehow independently wealthy, probably because she was born into wealth, and she helped fund Jesus' earthly ministry. She and a group of other women traveled with Jesus and His disciples, not only paying their way but also gleaning from His teachings and doing ministry alongside Him. She's mentioned *twelve times* in the Gospels, which may not seem like a lot, but it's more than any other woman in the New Testament, except Mary the mother of Jesus.

The most famous passage of Scripture including our girl MM is below, and I want us to read it slowly, picturing her face, her body, her voice, and what might have been going on in her soul as this story unfolded.

> Early in the morning on the first day of the week, while it was still dark, Mary Magdalene came to the tomb and saw that the stone was moved away from the entrance. She ran at once to Simon Peter and the other disciple,

the one Jesus loved, breathlessly panting, "They took the Master from the tomb. We don't know where they've put him."

Peter and the other disciple left immediately for the tomb. They ran, neck and neck. The other disciple got to the tomb first, outrunning Peter.

Stooping to look in, he saw the pieces of linen cloth lying there, but he didn't go in. Simon Peter arrived after him, entered the tomb, observed the linen cloths lying there, and the kerchief used to cover his head not lying with the linen cloths but separate, neatly folded by itself. Then the other disciple, the one who had gotten there first, went into the tomb, took one look at the evidence, and believed. No one yet knew from the Scripture that he had to rise from the dead. The disciples then went back home.

It's important for us to remember, when reading this passage, that the idea of Jesus rising from the dead and the tomb being empty is one we've been hearing for over two thousand years. We can only imagine the confusion, the shock, and the fear that these people probably felt when they discovered the body of their friend was missing. This can help us understand why Mary is about to react the way she does:

But Mary stood outside the tomb weeping. As she wept, she knelt to look into the tomb and saw two angels sitting there, dressed in white, one at the head, the other at the foot of where Jesus' body had been laid. They said to her, "Woman, why do you weep?"

"They took my Master," she said, "and I don't know where they put him." After she said this, she turned away and saw Jesus standing there. But she didn't recognize him.

Jesus spoke to her, "Woman, why do you weep? Who are you looking for?"

She, thinking that he was the gardener, said, "Mister, if you took him, tell me where you put him so I can care for him."

Jesus said, "Mary."

Turning to face him, she said in Hebrew, "*Rabboni!*" meaning "Teacher!"

Jesus said, "Don't cling to me, for I have not yet ascended to the Father. Go to my brothers and tell them, 'I ascend to my Father and your Father, my God and your God.'"

Mary Magdalene went, telling the news to the disciples: "I saw the Master!" And she told them everything he said to her. (John 20:1–18 MSG)

First: I pray you've heard Him call your name like that. I pray you've perceived His specific acknowledgement. If you never have, you can pray right now that you would. Maybe we don't all hear the audible voice of God, but I do believe the Holy Spirit speaks to our souls in a really specific and tangible way. I'm praying for you, right now, even as I write, that you'd experience God in this way.

Now, where to start with Mary? Her faithfulness, to relentlessly care for this man from whom she'd been learning? We also know she was one of the few present at His crucifixion (see John 19:25) when most of the disciples had either retreated in fear, denied knowing Jesus, or were watching from afar. Mary has bided her time, being faithful to rest on the Sabbath, and is now at Jesus' tomb, to continue serving Him in His supposed death before the sun has even risen. *Yes, Mary is faithful.*

She's also humble and incredibly loyal. The words she used to refer to Jesus, even when she supposes Him to still be dead, illustrate this. She uses the words Κύριος ἐγώ, (kurios egó) which mean "the master of me," to describe who she believes Jesus to be. When she does recognize Him, she greets Him by saying, "Rabboni!"

I've learned to stop and take note any time the Bible gives us someone's words in Aramaic. It was the language everyone spoke in Israel at the time, Jesus included, and when these accounts were translated to Greek later on, there were a few words and phrases that were too significant to translate into a different language. So instead, in some translations of the Bible, we get the actual Aramaic quote and a deeper meaning of what was said. Some of those references include Jesus crying out to the Father on the cross (Mark 15:34) or declarative moments of healing (Mark 5:41). We can assume there isn't a Greek word complex enough to help us understand what *Rabboni* meant, so the word remains in Aramaic.

It's respectful and intimate all at once. It's teacher and master, yet with personal implications of relationship. This word is referenced only one other time in the New Testament—by a blind man who asks Jesus to heal him. This is how that conversation goes down in Mark 10, in the New American Standard Version (NASB) of the Bible:

And answering him, Jesus said, "What do you want Me to do for you?" And the blind man said to Him, "[Rabboni,

I want to regain my sight!" And Jesus said to him, "Go; your faith has made you well." Immediately he regained his sight and began following Him on the road.

Sometimes I wonder if the act of the blind man calling Jesus "Rabboni" was what demonstrated his faith in a way that compelled Jesus to heal him. It's a strong word, and it's the one Mary Magdalene chooses to embrace her Savior with when she sees Him after the darkest few days on earth. *Mary is faithful, and she is personally connected to Jesus. He is her teacher, friend, master, and Savior.*

That's not all, folks! My favorite parts about Mary are still ahead.

Let's look again at what an incredible task her Savior, Friend, Master, Healer, and Redeemer entrusts her with:

Jesus said, "Mary."

Turning to face him, she said in Aramaic, "*Rabboni!*" meaning "Teacher!"

Jesus said, "Don't cling to me, for I have not yet ascended to the Father. Go to my brothers and tell them, 'I ascend to my Father and your Father, my God and your God.'"

Mary Magdalene went, telling the news to the disciples: "I saw the Master!" And she told them everything he said to her. (John 20:16–18 MSG)

Another name biblical historians call Mary of Magdala is "the apostle to the apostles."* She was the first person entrusted

---

* Maurice Casey, *Jesus of Nazareth: An Independent Historian's Account of His Life and Teaching* (London: T & T Clark, 2010), 193.

with the news that Jesus was who He said He was, that all hope was not lost, and that help and redemption were on the way. I like to paraphrase this and say that Jesus told Mary, "GO AND TELL THE BOYS I'M UP," but I suppose His words are much more profound. I can't tell you how much it means to me as a believer and a sharer of the Good News that Jesus was so intentional in allowing a woman to be the first one to relay the message that He had risen.

So I'm wondering, *Who was this woman?* What kind of woman gets the honor of so much airtime in the Bible? What kind of woman gets the massive privilege of serving alongside Jesus, funding His earthly ministry, seeing His moves up close? What kind of woman is hand-picked to have the first post-resurrection moment with Him, to be the first to proclaim the good news that He is alive?

What kind of woman?

We're heading to one more passage, but before we transition to another book of the Bible, let's make a distinction between the Gospels. I don't know if we're supposed to have a favorite Gospel account (between the four, Matthew, Mark, Luke, and John), but they're pretty varied, and for good reason. Each of the Gospels was written from a different man's perspective, and each of those men was called to a different people group and purpose, much like we are. To me, that makes the small differences and variations in the Gospels that much more beautiful to look at as a whole. John's account, which we've been looking at for Mary's story, is often very emotional and personal—he was interested in the personal connection to Jesus everyone had, and I love that. For this reason, John is one of my favorite Gospels. But my tip-top favorite is Luke. Luke was a doctor who was writing to someone named Theophilus to get eyewitness accounts of what in the world was going on and why everyone was talking about this Jesus. I'll tell you more about why I love Luke in chapter 16.

But first, I tend to love what Luke wrote because he was very facts-driven. He wouldn't put pen to paper unless several eyewitness accounts had confirmed something. I love Luke because, while I'm an emotional girl and John pulls at my heartstrings, I'm also prone to doubt. I know that if Luke wrote it, I can trust it, because he was a meticulous fact-finder and historical accuracy was of utmost importance to him. So this next passage is from Luke, though the fact I most want you to gather is also confirmed in the book of Mark.

This is Mary's introduction in the book of Luke:

After this, Jesus traveled about from one town and village to another, proclaiming the good news of the kingdom of God. The Twelve were with him, and also some women who had been cured of evil spirits and diseases: *Mary (called Magdalene) from whom seven demons had come out*; Joanna the wife of Chuza, the manager of Herod's household; Susanna; and many others. These women were helping to support them out of their own means. (Luke 8:1–3)

Mary Magdalene. Friend of Jesus. Supporter of His ministry. Apostle to the apostles. First human to see the resurrected Jesus and first to tell the good news of all His claims and promises being made true. What kind of woman gets that kind of privilege in the kingdom of God?

One who'd had seven demons cast out of her.

DEEP DEVOTION

If you've been around the church for a while or read the Bible, this probably doesn't surprise you. Maybe you've grown used to Jesus picking the least likely, or maybe even His radical grace has grown stale in your heart. You know that this is what He does: makes broken things beautiful again and again and again. Takes the weak and makes them strong, blah blah blah. Sister, can you go take a lap around your house or do a headstand or something? I need you to shake it up and remember that this is *not normal*.

In our churches and faith communities today, we can't relate to this. The most busted and broken people of the group *do not get chosen* to lead the whole shebang. Most of us have lost the strength to believe He can actually heal the messiest stories. The woman in our church who just might have seven demons messing with her? For most of our churches, she's too disruptive. We draw boundaries with her and don't invite her to our coffee dates. We certainly don't ask her to *lead*.

Maybe we need a quick shake in order to remember that when the transformative power of Jesus Christ meets painfully dark and heavy brokenness, He doesn't just *slightly* clean it up. He doesn't merely do some tidying. He doesn't sweep the grossest stuff under the rug. And He never, ever passes by brokenness in order to play with the more manageable kids on the playground.

This is an important moment, as we're beginning to believe and apply the truth that Jesus has called *us* to be the girls for the job. Can we pause and check whether or not we believe that truth applies to those who are most entrenched in sin, affliction, suffering—who are the most downtrodden amongst us? Do we believe that when His grace and glory meet their neediness, they are *also* the girls for the job? And will we be the ones to tell them that?

Now, for those of you who feel like Mary before Jesus got his hands on those demons, I've got a word.

First: there is no doubt in my mind that you're the girl for the job. There is no doubt in my mind that you've gotten this book on purpose. I believe someone prayed it into your hands or gave it to you intentionally. No matter when in the future you're reading this, I am praying right now as I write that the God of the Universe will orchestrate you having it on the day you most need it, the day you least believe that He loves you and wants to use you.

I want you to know that I've been the girl who can't stop crying in the back row at church. I've been the one ostracized for being honest about what afflicts me. I've had leaders of small groups call my husband and say, "I know you're going through a rough time, but if Jessi can't stop crying during group, it might be better if she doesn't come. It's bringing the group down, and it's reflecting poorly on you as a husband." I've been the one grieving, the one struggling with depression. I've been the one with the sick kid, the one with the autoimmune disease that will never leave. And I might not know your exact situation—what keeps you feeling like you're too much for humans and too broken for God to use you—but I know that His capacity plus our willingness always equals abundance. I do not think you're the exception.

Bart D. Ehrman, a New Testament scholar and historian of early Christianity, has some serious spiritual insight into Mary and her seven demons. Let's pay attention:

The number seven may be merely symbolic, since, in Jewish tradition, seven was the number of completion, so the statement that Mary was possessed by seven demons may simply mean she was completely overwhelmed by their power. In either case, Mary must have suffered from *severe emotional or psychological trauma* in order for an exorcism of this kind to have been perceived as necessary. *Consequently, her devotion to Jesus on account of this healing must have been very strong.* The gospel-writers normally relish giving dramatic descriptions of Jesus' public exorcisms, with the possessed person wailing, thrashing, and tearing his or her clothes in front of a crowd. The fact that Mary's exorcism is given so little attention may indicate that it was *either done in private or that it was not seen as particularly dramatic.**

A few things to catch here:

- Whether she had seven demons at once, seven demons over seven years, or she was just really messed with by some demons, Mary was a woman who obviously knew trauma.
- Um, yes. For so many of us, there is a direct correlation between the strength of the bondage that we've been set free from and the strength of our devotion to the One who freed us. It makes perfect sense that Mary was one of Jesus' most devoted followers, amen?
- Though many exorcisms and healings are told about in the Bible, Mary's is not, and I can't help but wonder if that's because Jesus wanted to give His friend a little

---

* Bart D. Ehrman, *Peter, Paul, and Mary Magdalene: The Followers of Jesus in History and Legend* (Oxford, England: Oxford University Press, 2006), 229.

privacy. Her past wasn't hidden, but it didn't need to define her. Mary's story was not her exorcism—her story was her especially beautiful friendship with Jesus.

This is what we agree with in our brains but don't always display in our communities: the greater the brokenness we've been brought out of, the deeper our devotion to Jesus, who did the bringing out.

Am I saying you can't have a powerful ministry if you haven't been possessed by demons, struggled with addictions, lost people close to you, lived through sin, or done dramatic damage to those around you? Absolutely not.

We'd be wise to remember that all brokenness and sin keeps us separated from a holy and perfect God. Romans 3:23 tells us that all fall short of the glory of God, and Romans 3:10 reminds us that no one is holy. Romans 2:11 says that God shows no partiality. Whether your life has looked like a mess or been nice and tidy, the truth remains: you need Jesus. And the more we allow ourselves to perceive His grace, the more we'll experience His power.

WE'VE GOT A POWER PROBLEM

But he said to me, "My grace is sufficient for you, for my power is made perfect in weakness." Therefore I will boast all the more gladly about my weaknesses, so that Christ's power may rest on me. (2 Corinthians 12:9)

Here's where we stand so far in this book:

We're holding both the bad news that the world is in major need of help and the good news that God has put us here on purpose. We've quit (or we're actively trying to quit) striving to be the best, and we've put God back on the throne—remember, He's the One worthy of worship anyhow. We kissed our ideal selves goodbye and thanked them for what they taught us, and then we moved on to really allowing ourselves to see those around us as the motivator for our mission.

But before we take another step forward, let's place a dilemma on the table. We're going to need energy, strength, and stamina to step into a life of loving and serving others, much less to keep going. If I'm being honest, my actual, normal life of maintenance takes all that I've got. To pay my bills, to feed my kids, to exercise, to wash the sheets occasionally, to water the plants, to show up at church, to serve semi-regularly, to buy groceries, and to take my vitamins—that's a full life. Left to my own devices, I won't have the power I need to even *think* about anyone else as I'm living my everyday life.

Unless it comes from a supernatural place. Unless I'm truly motivated by something miraculous that happened in me and which I want to happen for others. Unless, like Mary Magdalene, I've experienced some deep and beautiful healing and I'm dead set on doing what I can to make sure everyone else knows this Teacher, this Master, this Friend of mine.

Here's what Scripture tells us about Mary: she financially supported Jesus in ministry, which gives us cause to believe she was born into an affluent family. In the matriarchal society of the New Testament, much would have been expected of her regarding homemaking and family maintenance. And yet she was compelled by something greater—a power that was made perfect in her weakness, a calling that was initiated in her own brokenness. There was more than a life of maintenance in store for Mary because she took Jesus at His Word and wanted other people to see what she'd seen.

I don't know about you. I don't know if you're the gal in the back row of the church who can't stop crying or if you've lived the tidiest life imaginable. I don't know if you've been rebuked for allowing your brokenness to be seen or if you've never let another human being in on it for fear of rejection.

But I do know the kind of woman Mary was, and I do know the kind of women Jesus loves to use for His glory and their good, and I know where our power comes from. Can we pause now and ask God for a new way, a new strength, a new system to be energized for what's ahead? One that isn't based on our accolades or empowering phrases that pump us up? Can we ask God for real, unending, Spirit-filled power from on high that comes only when we let His light invade our darkness over and over and over again? Can we trust our friend Jesus, and let Him see where we're coming from and what we're working with—even the parts of our hearts and lives that we've hidden from the rest of the world?

Let's confirm, aided by the Word of God and the Spirit of Truth, that we're the kind of women God uses because we're open and eager to have His healing meet our brokenness. Let's confirm, once again, that we are the girls for the job, not because of the successes of our past but because of the strength of His saving grace. And let's be women who confirm for every other sister in Christ, no matter what her brokenness, that she's the kind of woman God uses, too.

CHAPTER 8

GOD HAS THE LAST WORD IN YOUR WEAKNESS

Have you ever done something, said something, so wrong that you immediately wanted to hide?

That was me yesterday, literally, as of this writing.

Yesterday, I found myself on a walk with two of my children, one of whom will remain nameless for their protection. This one child, whom I love so dearly, was being kind of awful to me, and had been for a prolonged period of time. After much berating and heckling from this one very passionate and headstrong child, I lost it. I mom-lost it. I turned around and just lost it. And by lost it, I mean I directed a four-letter word, for the very first time, at one of my kids. Some of you might think I'm the worst sort of mom for this, and some of you might think I'm a saint for having made it eleven years without doing such a thing, but the truth is, I was pretty shocked at myself. I was ashamed. I wanted to hide.

Yelling is my *struggle*. And *anger* is my greatest enemy, but never before had it bubbled over into actually cursing at one of my kids.

Almost as soon as I said it, I turned away, covered my head with my hands, took a deep breath, and turned back.

"Sweetheart," I said. "I'm really sorry. I just got so angry and I lost my temper and I said something I really shouldn't have said. You also shouldn't have been talking to me that way, but I need to ask you to forgive me."

The thing I love about the kid with whom I was having this exchange is that they're super feisty and stubborn. I know God is going to use that tenacity one day to fight for and change the world, but in this moment, it was directed at me and *it was unrelenting*. The child actually refused to forgive me, and instead continued to yell at and berate me for using such language. I was over yelling and anger at this point, so I calmly called Nick to come pick up this kid up from the walk, since we were not doing each other any favors at this point. Nick came, they went home, the kid later apologized (after cooling off), and I apologized again for my extremely inappropriate language.

But my son Elias and I kept walking, and here's what transpired:

ELIAS: Mom, are you okay?

ME: Yeah, bud. I'm so sorry that happened. I'm so sorry I got so angry. Will you forgive me?

ELIAS: Of course, mom. Honestly, I would have gotten that angry too.

ME: Well, if you ever do get that angry at someone, please learn from me and pick better words or walk away.

ELIAS: I actually learned so much from you just now. Because you stopped and apologized.

ME: [Gently flicking away tears and trying not to cry.]

ELIAS: I think the most important thing in the world we can know is God. And the second most important thing we can know is our weaknesses. And you know this is your weakness, and you stopped and apologized. And so today, I learned how to not let your weakness control you.

I promise with all that's in me that this kid doesn't even know what this book is about, much less the fact that I'm about to write a chapter based on the very words he's just said, words highlighting the principle on which I've tried to base my life.

And I promise that if I thought we could move on already, into your dreams and strengths and plans for loving the world around you, I would, but there are a few reasons I believe Elias is incredibly right about how important it is that we know our weaknesses and hold them like weapons against the darkness.

YOUR WEAKNESS IS REAL

The first is this: *Your weakness is real. But I don't believe in blaming or hiding, unless it's in the cross of Christ. As we take steps forward, believing He's placed us here on purpose for the good of others and the glory of God—we cannot go boldly and hide at the same time.*

We have a lot to learn. *I* have a lot to learn. Because the most natural human response in the world, when faced with our weakness, is to hide.

We see this in the very beginning of God's relationship with man and woman, as Adam and Eve are faced with the temptation to ignore God's simple request for obedience:

> When the Woman saw that the tree looked like good eating and realized what she would get out of it—she'd know everything!—she took and ate the fruit and then gave some to her husband, and he ate.
>
> Immediately the two of them did "see what's really going on"—saw themselves naked! They sewed fig leaves together as makeshift clothes for themselves. When they heard the sound of God strolling in the garden in the evening breeze, the Man and his Wife hid in the trees of the garden, hid from God.
>
> God called to the Man: "Where are you?" He said, "I heard you in the garden and I was afraid because I was naked. And I hid."
>
> God said, "Who told you you were naked? Did you eat from that tree I told you not to eat from?" The Man said, "The Woman you gave me as a companion, she gave me fruit from the tree, and, yes, I ate it."
>
> God said to the Woman, "What is this that you've done?"
>
> "The serpent seduced me," she said, "and I ate."
> (Genesis 3:6–13 MSG)

Both Adam and Eve hid from God when faced with their sin, and both chose to blame someone else rather than taking responsibility.

My friend, I don't know where your weaknesses came from. I'm not sure if you've spent time tracing their roots, identifying when they first made their appearance. When it comes to yelling at my kids, I remember the first time I ever felt the rush of unholy power and truly *screamed* at them. I know the seed of sin that is anger was already in my heart, and I know I was already someone who had to watch how I used my words, because I was very liable to hurt someone. I'd been a yeller in my life, but I'd never, *never* yelled at my kids before the early summer of 2011.

It was sometime just after Father's Day, and I know the timing so well because on Mother's Day of that year, I found out I was pregnant, and on Father's Day, I found out I was miscarrying. The next few weeks were extremely painful both physically and emotionally, as my body didn't want to miscarry naturally, and I needed a lot of intervention and help from doctors. I was in so much pain, and suddenly, being alone with our kids was so much harder because I couldn't chase after our sweet four-, three-, and two-year-olds. One day, when they were just being kids and I had to get their attention, I screamed. In anger. And it worked. And I kept yelling.

This moment has become a historical event in my life, because it pinpoints my choice to act on this sin of mine. And honestly, yelling at my kids is still one of my biggest active weaknesses. But I certainly can't blame the miscarriage for my sin of yelling *today*, the same way it doesn't help me to blame any other human for any other decision or agreement I make with my mind, body, or words.

It's our natural inclination to shift the blame for our major weaknesses onto others. We can find fault with those who excelled and caused us to stumble in the shadow of their light. We can find fault with just about anyone who played a role in the development of the darker parts of our personality or character—the areas we wish we could leave behind.

But it's our supernatural birthright, bought by the blood of Jesus and made possible by the power of the Holy Spirit, to quit blaming others for our weaknesses and instead allow the grace of God to transform them into something He can use for His glory and our good. We have been given the supernatural ability to let God use our weaknesses so His power can be made perfect in our lives. The days of blame are done; the days of redemption are here.

LET'S STOP HIDING

And what about hiding? We're not only breaking bonds of generational sin that started with Adam and Eve, we're going to war with cultural expectations and standards that have built fortresses of fear around the idea of simply being ourselves and being honest with our own struggles. Even today, even in a culture that is beginning to say, "Come as you are," it is wildly unacceptable to be weak. Especially in the church. Especially for believers.

On the flip side, I find that the incredibly brave souls who are comfortable sharing their weaknesses often have a "take it or leave it" mentality that screams, "Here is my ugly side. Embrace it! Love it! Don't touch it! It's mine!" And while the bravery to bring forth the truth is worth applauding and encouraging, this mind-set leaves no room for God's power to find its true purpose in redemption. To own our weaknesses but not allow any growth to come from them is like receiving the best gift in the world and refusing to open it.

We don't have to live as women who continue in cycles of hiding and blame anymore, and we don't have to be women who are complicit in allowing other women to slip into these same shame-inducing patterns. We can be freedom fighters for the women around us when we go first, open up, share our own truth—weaknesses, warts, *and* redemption. We can literally change the world by being a safe place for others when we allow women to own the darkest parts of their lives and then encourage them to let the light transform them by the power of the Holy Spirit.

LET'S CHANGE THE WORLD

Have you ever wanted to change the world? I have three words for you: say you're sorry.

If we don't have to hide, we might as well 'fess up. Go ahead and publicly repent. This isn't weakness; it is our witness. It is our worship. And when we own the things we genuinely could have done better and experience God's grace, it frees up others to do the same.

So let's stop hiding our weaknesses from God and other people, and, fueled by grace and compelled to change, drop the weapon of blame right where we currently stand. Don't take that tool forward with you; it's not the one you want. Have you ever wanted to *drastically* change the world? Let a friend show you *her* weaknesses and don't back away. Don't try to tidy her up, fix her, or convince her that what she showed you isn't all that bad. Honor her honesty with care and the belief that God wants to use her weaknesses to grow her, mold her, and make her into the woman she was created to be.

Why are we *still* talking about weaknesses and all the potentially negative sides of this call that's been placed on your life? Because to be completely honest, it's the hiding and the blame that will keep you from stepping into God's abundance more than anything else. The Word of God proves to us over and over again that weaknesses will not keep us from obediently fulfilling whatever the Father has for us. But if we do not bring our whole selves to the table, we will not receive the fullness of His power. And if our hearts are embittered by blame, we won't be freed up to love the people we've been asked to.

REDEFINING WEAKNESS

I have a theory about what we talk about when we talk about our weaknesses. Here it is: *When we don't own up and apologize for our real weaknesses, we end up apologizing for qualities that aren't weaknesses at all.*

Let me show you what I mean:

Independent.
Strong-willed.
Outspoken.
Meek.
Humble.

Honest.
Aloof.
Excitable.
Enthusiastic.

These are simply personality traits. They're not inherently negative or positive. Yet across the world, these descriptors are being used both to praise women and demean them. Why is it good in some contexts to be known as outspoken and independent, and bad in other contexts? Why can't we agree on these traits?

It would be foolish for me to attempt to dive in and prescribe personality characteristics for anyone, so instead I'll just caution you to hold your "weaknesses" up to the Word of God and see what He says about them. Ask whether or not these are attributes found in the character of Christ, in whose image we've been made.

Before you spend one more moment bemoaning your perceived shortcomings, it would be wildly helpful to identify if they actually make you weak or if they make you more like Christ. You are the girl for the job because you've been created intentionally and held together miraculously and mercifully by a God who loves you, sees you, and hopes the best in you. Your weaknesses are not a liability to the kingdom of God, and there is no skeleton in the closet or hidden trait in your being that would shock Him or cause Him to stop coming toward you in grace. All of you is loved, all of you is held, everything is redeemable, and the rest of your life is dependent on *His* capacity, not your ability to cover up who you are or how you've been made.

You are the girl for the job.

Not in spite of your weaknesses, but because His power is made perfect in them.

CHAPTER 9

THE BEST GIFT EVER

IT'S ABOUT THE GIVER

Do you know your love languages? Gary Chapman first wrote about the five love languages in his 1995 book, *The Five Love Languages: How to Express Heartfelt Commitment to Your Mate.* And I, for one, am incredibly grateful for this helpful tool. The premise is that most people desire to receive love in one or two particular ways, they tend to give love in one or two particular ways, and it's important that we know our natural propensity when it comes to how we give love and how we desire to receive it.

It's a crazy helpful tool, not just for marriages, but for friendships and parenting. I'm thankful for the way it's helped me see the people I love and evaluate how they're doing. The different love languages are words of affirmation, physical touch, acts of service, gifts, and quality time.

Three out of my four kids *need* to be touched every day, even the older two, who are approaching their tween years and may not ask to cuddle or may not initiate a hug. They need me to come for them with a cuddle before bed, a pat on the back, or a big squeeze before they get out of the car for school. That's how they receive love, and if I go too many days without giving it to them, I see them get a little ornery. The fourth kid would be fine with never being touched but craves quality time and gifts like nobody I've ever met.

My husband and I have mismatching love languages, and that right there is a big old bummer. Let me explain: I tend to give love by offering words of affirmation, and that's also how I like to receive love. Nick loves by acts of service, which means very little to me. I mean, it doesn't mean *nothing*, but if I don't pay careful attention, I won't realize just how much he's doing to serve me all day long. I won't see how sacrificial and gracious he's being. Likewise, words of encouragement don't mean that much to him, so he has a tendency to discount them if he's not careful. He'd much rather have quality time.

If we're not intentional, we can miss each other's displays of affections altogether, both feeling unloved and unseen, when really, we're both trying to be loving and kind. Our opportunity is to slow down long enough to notice how others are trying to love us and hope the best in their attempts and intent. We also have the opportunity to be wildly intentional in the way that we love—asking the hard question: Is this what I want to do, or is this what they need?

This summer, I've been in the thick of writing this book while also trying to "summer well" with my kiddos. This has looked like early mornings of writing followed by long days of play, while also trying to get to bed on time so I can get up early and write again. It's been exhausting, but oh-so-worth-it, and one of our favorite ways to play has been board games. Risk,

Monopoly, and, in particular, Scrabble have taken up a large chunk of our summer, and I'm not mad about it.

There were a few mornings in a row where I'd come out from the bedroom at 5 a.m. ready to write but dragging from the past day. Then, to my delight, I'd see a gift on the table from my husband. The Scrabble board, still out from the night before, would be arranged in a little love note for me. Simple phrases like "I love you" or "Keep writing" were arranged using the white letter tiles, and as I saw them with my cloudy morning eyes, I'd break out in the world's biggest smile. I would tell Nick later in the day how much it meant to me, how encouraged those little gifts left me as I started writing. He paid attention.

Our thirteenth wedding anniversary was a few weeks later, and Nick seemed so excited about the gift he had for me. I was blessed to unwrap a Scrabble board with letter tiles glued down, permanently stuck in an arrangement he'd created. All the words filling the board were encouragements—attributes he wanted to affirm over me: leader, writer, passionate, loving, mother, kind, strong, beautiful.

The gift was the best ever because it was the one I needed. Because it was specifically tailored to me, my personality and emotional needs. I felt seen by him, the giver, and loved and known.

I honestly don't deserve a lot of those words. The gift speaks much more of Nick than it does of me. It speaks of his intention, his grace, and his generosity. And so forever and always, that Scrabble board is going to mean a ton to me. It tells me who my husband is and reminds me of his ability to see me and my emotional needs. It reminds me of his ability to affirm who God made me to be.

If you think about it, the gift always speaks more about the giver than the receiver. When I tell you about that—about the intentionality and the thoughtfulness behind the Scrabble board—you probably don't think, *Wow, she must just be so impressive to inspire such a gift.*

No, you're just straight-up impressed by my husband right now. Just like I was! And that's my point: a great gift says far more about the giver than the receiver.

Likewise, God has given you a set of gifts. He has very specifically designed a set of strengths within you, with full knowledge of how they'd develop and how you would utilize them. He crafted each skill and every competence with purpose, with you in mind, not only for your good but for how you will benefit others with them. And He's kept His own glory at the forefront of His objective, as that will always be the main goal of giving any of His kids gifts in the first place.

Before we spend even one more moment talking about the gifts our Father has carefully imparted to you, I want to take a moment to remember together that when we talk about the gifts, it's the Giver we really get to focus on.

To discount what He's given you, to neglect what our Father has planted inside of you, would essentially be to stiff-arm the Giver of all good gifts. So let's call it quits on that right now.

Do not neglect your gift, which was given you through prophecy when the body of elders laid their hands on you. Be diligent in these matters; give yourself wholly to them, so that everyone may see your progress. Watch your life and doctrine closely. Persevere in them, because if you do, you will save both yourself and your hearers. (1 Timothy 4:14–16)

The Giver has given you an intentional set of strengths, and to shirk them, to hide them, to let them atrophy is the opposite of worship. *It is honoring to our Father when you acknowledge what He's given you for the good of others and for His glory.*

To stand woefully before Him and all the people He's placed in front of us to serve and mourn that we don't seem to have any gifts—that's calling Him a bad giver. That's the same as calling Him careless or thoughtless or insinuating He has the capacity to skip over one of us, and all that I know to be true of God tells me He can't forget even one of His kids. He *wouldn't* forget one of His kids.

The Giver has not forgotten you, and He has not passed over you. *It's time to look with expectation and hopeful eyes, ready to see the strengths our Father has intentionally placed inside you, because I know that I know that they're there.*

As well, to see our gifts and strengths as our accomplishments or as capacities we've built ourselves is wildly lacking in humility and acknowledgement of His love, affection, and work in our lives.

It's not humble to pretend He didn't give us gifts or to pretend that we're responsible for the gifts. We need to and we get to give credit where it's due and use what He's given, when He asks us to, for His glory.

Again, the gifts are less about the character of the recipient and more about the Giver. Let's keep that straight in our heads and in our hearts as we move forward.

I NEVER GOT ANYTHING

A friend and I were debating this the other day: Is it that many of us don't *know* what our gifts are, or is it that we don't *like* what they are? Maybe, in different seasons, it's both. Perhaps you wish you could trade with a friend and get a little of what she's been given. Maybe you have no hesitation identifying the strengths God has placed in your life. If that's the case, it's my absolute joy to tell you to either read this section to be able to encourage your friends or to skip it entirely.

Here are some of my favorite tips and tricks for being on the lookout for the gifts God has given you. I invite you to go on a treasure hunt, looking for His grace and goodness expressed *to* you and *through* you. Go humbly, and go gratefully, remembering that none of this is about you or your glory—that's why you're safe to look for His hand at work in your life. This is not a quest to figure out how awesome you are, it's an intentional investigation that will allow you to be in awe of God in your own life. *You ready?*

Phone a Friend

Let's go with the most vulnerable option first, since we're such brave women who are girded by the breastplate of righteousness and guarded by the shield of our faith. You only need one honest and gracious friend for this exercise to work, but you can always go to two or three if you've got them. My encouragement is to be humble and honest and say some version of the following, if it feels true for you:

Hi. I would like to have a kind of strange conversation with you.

I'm on a hunt to find out how God has gifted me, to discover what strengths He has given me. I'm wildly aware of my weaknesses, and I know what most of my biggest struggles are. If you'd like to speak into those, I'm open to it, but let's leave that for another conversation. I'm trying to determine my strengths so I can use them for His glory and the good of others.

You know me. You see me live and move and work in this world.

Would you help me figure out the gifts He's given me?

It might take some time and that's okay. If you know some off the bat, awesome. If you need to watch and pay attention, that's cool too. I'll be praying that God gives us both eyes to see. And I'd love to speak into *your* strengths as well. Thanks, friend.

Phone a friend. Give her space to think it over and grace to notice things you never would. Invite her to join you on this quest to step into God's great and beautiful call on your life.

Listen, I'm fine if you just want to send her a screenshot of the above paragraph. That's also acceptable. Or you could just buy her this book, and then she'll have read the whole lead-up, and you'll both be poised for this abundant treasure hunt.

A disclaimer: out of all of the women who read this book, I imagine there will be some of you who try this exercise and have a friend who doesn't respond well. She may not understand; she may think it's extra or silly. She may call you prideful or selfish or say something hurtful when you were looking for encouragement.

Can I exhort you to show her grace and be patient with her

if this mind-set is new for her? I'm not suggesting you stay in an unhealthy relationship or continually invite someone who tends to be hurtful to speak into the most tender parts of your heart. I am, however, suggesting that we allow people to grow, and this exercise—and really, this whole adventure we're on, to believe that we are the girls for the job—isn't easy for everyone. You've had eight chapters to gear up for this, so my encouragement is to show her a little grace if it feels foreign to her.

Use Your Eyes

If you're asking for her help, you're going to have to carry your weight, too, sister-friend. I'm believing that our strong and competent Father will give you eyes to see and ears to hear exactly what you need to. What are you already doing in your everyday life that is blessing others and changing the world? What comes naturally to you that doesn't to others? Are there ways you serve, bless, love, or lead—maybe rhythms or processes that are more automatic for you? If we're believing that God is the giver of all good gifts, then that means we believe these aren't descriptions of how you're just naturally *better* than others—these are specific gifts He's given you to enact His rescue plan of love where you're at.

What seems to help the people around you? What do you wish more people would help you do? These are God-given gifts, and you are the girl for the job.

And, *what do you delight in?*

God is most glorified when we are most satisfied in Him. John Piper coined this question in his book *Desiring God*, and it shook my early Christian life in a beautiful and refreshing way. It was mind-blowing for me to hear the truth that I was allowed to and encouraged to *enjoy* life in Christ. There was no guarantee that life would suddenly get tidy, manageable, or easy, but there was something better wrapped up in the idea of abundance: delight, wonder, comfort, and an at-ease-ness are mine for the taking when the Lord and I are in communion.

In the name of Jesus, I'd like to tell you the great news that the same is true for the daughters of God when we use our strengths and gifts for His glory. When we've given up on the idea of fame and appreciation for our own sakes, when we've truly considered the good of those around us, after we push through all our fears about being obedient and pick up the tools placed inside us by a good Father, abundance comes. Joy comes. Freedom comes. And we might just *savor* utilizing our strengths.

So, friend, are there ways you serve that leave you with feelings of delight and joy? I realize it's not always about the warm fuzzies, and that this doesn't mean that we're on a quest to use our strengths for our own pleasure, but let's not be confused. When we are obedient and operating out of His grace and strength, joy *will* come.

Do you *love* to write? Do your fingers itch and ache with the desire to swiftly tap out words of exhortation and encouragement? Girl, write.

Do you come alive teaching the Word of God? Does it get your heart racing to see faces in front of you waking up to the beauty of God's Word? Friend, grab your Bible, and let's go.

Does making a plan give you butterflies? Does developing systems and structures get you excited? Do you love the simplicity of serving children? Do those things.

If arranging flowers brings you joy, do it to the glory of God.

If cutting hair makes you smile, run on mission and cut every head of hair you can, encouraging every person who sits in your chair.

As you're asking God to help you see the strengths, gifts, talents, and areas where you are gifted, please don't ignore the areas of life that bring you joy and satisfaction. God is most glorified when you are most satisfied in Him, and this does not exclude the immense joy and satisfaction that can come when we serve others in the ways He created us to do so. Listen to your life: What makes you come alive? Seek to serve God with your gifts right here.

Go Back to Your Weaknesses

Often, if I'm talking with a friend who is having a hard time identifying her strengths and gifts, it helps to bring up what people have criticized about her in the past. It's not because I want to drum up painful memories, but because our advantages are often hidden in or masked by our disadvantages. Our assets, used in the wrong way or even toward the wrong person at the wrong time, are often seen and identified as liabilities.

More than I am an author or a speaker, I'm a communicator. Your girl likes to talk. I like to communicate ideas, feelings, and emotions, and God has made me a conduit of those concepts. I am gifted at transmitting what is in my head to those who are listening. How do I know? Because I've hurt many feelings. I know I'm a gifted communicator because the temptation is always present for me to manipulate others with my emotions. I'm aware of my capacity to use my tone, inflection, and emotive words because I once had a friend tell me that if we were in a heated discussion on the phone, and one of her kids could hear my voice, they would instinctively start crying. Am I proud of that? Am I grateful that my words, in written and oral form, have been used as a weapon to hurt or wound children of God? No. I'm incredibly broken over that. But!

I'm faced with a choice: Do I bury my communication gift deep beneath the surface, giving into the fear of using it the wrong way, *or* do I keep exposing it to the light, grace, and power of the gospel so I can learn to use my words for good?

If you're looking for strengths, don't look too far past your weaknesses, because chances are you'll find some important clues there. Your humility may present itself as shyness, your gift of leadership could have come to the surface under the cloak of bossiness, and your gift of mercy may have been masked and labeled as being too tenderhearted.

But we know better, women of God, when we believe and affirm that we were made in the image of God, wonderfully and fearfully. We don't stand with our eyes closed and our fingers in our ears, unwilling to admit we can make a mistake. Rather, we hold our entire selves—our personalities, pursuits, passions, and attributes—up to our good Father, who brings them under His authority for the sake of His glory and the good of others.

Your strengths may have been seen as weaknesses, or they may have even been used as weapons in a negative capacity, but they don't have to stay that way.

YOU'RE NOT STUCK

After all those suggestions to find the lane of your God-given strength or gift, I hope you have at least one idea in your mind of a way He's created you to love and serve others. Some of you might have twelve ideas, and some of you might be scared to say the sole strength that is rolling around in your heart and mind right now.

Now comes the paramount reminder that I pray you'll keep at the forefront of your mind:

You're not stuck in that strength forever.

First, God is too good and too wild to only give you one usable gift for the duration of your life. He's too creative and compelling to hand you only one tool. This is not your only strength, and it won't be the only gift you get from Him. Amen?

Second, this gift isn't the only one you have to use! Don't believe the lie that if you're a communicator, you can only impact people by communicating. Don't believe that if He's made you to be a leader, you can never change the world by quiet service. If He's placed in you the talent of singing for His glory, that doesn't exclude you from using your accounting skills to bless the world.

Let's not miss out on the abundance of God, the colors and the vibrancy He has to offer. Let's paint with every possible brush He will hand us for the rest of our lives. Nobody puts Baby in a corner (I'm referring here to the movie *Dirty Dancing*, for those of you born after 1985), and nobody tells the Jesus-loving daughters of the King that their Father is holding out on them. He doesn't have a scarcity mentality when it comes to you, so please don't adopt one.

All of you is perfectly designed by all of Him so that you can impact, grow, change, and ignite the world with His love *today*. Your past, your story, your weaknesses: they're allowed in your life on purpose. Your challenges, your triumphs, your strengths, your gifts: they've all been given to you so that more people can be exposed to the light of Christ. In the name of Jesus, let's open our eyes and see what we've been given. Let's call it good because He does. Let's take Him at His word that He'll equip us as we go, using what we've got. Amen?

FACE YOUR FEAR

Stop hiding, start fighting,
and demolish some strongholds.

CHAPTER 10

COME OUT, BIG ALICE

When I get together with my college roommates, there's one story we can't help but tell, retell, and laugh over every time we see each other. One night, during a beach trip, my friend Stephanie took the stairs instead of the elevator because she had a pretty extreme elevator phobia. We knew this about her—we lived in a dorm where she always took the stairs—but this night, for whatever reason, I was kind of harping on and on about it. I started telling the friends who had stayed with me how I couldn't think of anything I was truly scared of, except I was dead wrong, because I'm actually just scared of everything.

To be funny, Stephanie and the other gals had raced up the stairs and were waiting at the elevator on our floor, and they really gently said, "Boo!" when the doors opened. You can imagine the hilarity that ensued when the gal who was so aggressively declaring she wasn't scared of anything LOST HER MIND. I screamed, yelled, ran down the hall crying, and banged on our hotel door for someone to let me in because I was *so scared*.

In general, I am a person who knows fear. I have loved order, structure, and knowing what is next since birth, and some of my strongest childhood memories are not joy and wonder, but fear. Not because I had a horrific childhood, but because that's the way my brain operated in the past, letting my fear rise to the top, giving it the loudest microphone in my life.

I did the same thing a few years ago, the same hilarious denial trick that did not work, when I found Susie Davis' book *Unafraid*. Susie was a new acquaintance, one I adored, but I didn't feel the title or subject matter of her book resonated all that much with me. I mean, I couldn't think of anything on the surface of my life I was all that scared of. Note to self: when you can't think of one thing you're scared of, it may be wise to check and see if you're not just scared of everything. I got Susie's book around the time it came out, though, and I read it in forty-eight hours, sitting on my sofa as a weekend unfolded around me.

The hard shell I felt I needed in order to proclaim my courage melted off, and I started to realize how much fear was an ever-present banner over my heart and life.

> Though I don't know where your fears started or how deep they sit in your soul, I do know this: Fear is a heavy burden. One of the heaviest you can carry. It's exhausting and overwhelming. And it's not from God.*

Fast-forward to present day, and I want to be the first to hold my hands up in admission that I'm in the boat with you, needing the words that are about to come just as much as you do. My palms are up, and my eyes are on God, because I need a fresh session of facing my own fears so that the glory of God

---

* Susie Davis, *Unafraid: Trusting God in an Unsafe World* (Colorado Springs: WaterBrook Press, 2015).

can ring louder and truer, and so I can obediently move forward in all that He's called me to do.

But I'm not discouraged or beaten down because I know that these steps are worth repeating. I will take myself out of the running countless times for the rest of my life to keep God in the place He should be. I will obsess over those to whom He has called me to minister, asking the Holy Spirit to give me fresh vision and eyes to see who He's placed in my path. There will be moments scattered throughout the rest of my life when I'll have to consider my weaknesses and my strengths in the light of the call He's placed on my life. These steps, these processes, are worth repeating, so it's with a lot of expectancy and even joy that I start this chapter off with a confession.

Hi. I'm Jess. And I really struggle with fear.

I've got a specific set of things that are scaring me in this season, and I'd like to leave them behind as we work through this chapter together. I'm praying for you, and I'm praying for me, believing that the perfect love of our Father casts out fear. In the name of Jesus, I ask love to be louder in our hearts after we move on from this set of words. Amen?

WHAT IS BORN IN CAPTIVITY WILL NOT FLOURISH

I woke up the other night in a panic, retracing my dream, frantically splaying my fingers over my sheets, hair, and body to trigger my mind into the truth that I was awake and everything I'd just seen in my sleep wasn't real. I'd woken from a terrifying dream, but I also had a tinge of electrifying spiritual energy all around me: *there was something God wanted me to know about what I'd just seen.* So, in the stillness of 4 a.m., as I quietly climbed out of bed and made the rounds to check on my sleeping kids, I played back the dream in my mind.

Our family was on vacation, in some city I couldn't see or distinguish, and we'd just met up with a family we knew from the past. Together, all of us were going into some sort of mall that had a parking lot. In my dream, I had a sick feeling going into the parking lot. I knew something was wrong. We weren't supposed to go in there, so I told everyone to turn around, and I was grateful they listened. They knew we weren't supposed to go in there, either.

But as we were leaving, we saw a crime being committed, and the criminals spotted us. They said they couldn't let us go, so we'd have to come with them. We were being kidnapped—both families.

They took us to some underground living situation where we'd stay from now on, to keep us from sharing about the crime we'd seen. They used guns to keep us there in the beginning, but became less stringent over time. They'd leave the doors open, and the guns were nowhere to be found. We just stayed because we were scared of what would happen if we tried to leave.

Eventually, in my dream, the other family just left. One day, the mom decided she'd had enough, so she took her kids and walked right out, and the kidnappers didn't seem to notice. You'd think this would embolden me to leave, but it only assured me all the more that if we left, they'd come after us. We befriended the assailants, because it made it a more amicable place to live, and we tried to find the silver lining. Down here, in captivity, we had so much family time! We weren't busy!

Sure, we were living in a bunker and never saw sunshine, but we were together.

At the tail end of my dream, I could perceive that a lot of time had passed—our kids had grown older, and Nick and I were having another baby. I'd birthed the baby and was holding it, surrounded by Nick and the kids, which was so idyllic, except for the fact that we were kidnapped, living in a dungeon, and scared to leave.

Just after I saw the baby, I woke up, and as I replayed the dream in my mind, I heard the almost audible voice of God say this: *What is born into captivity cannot flourish.*

Things born into captivity cannot flourish. How can a baby born into a kidnapped family ever see the light of day or feel the wind on its face? Likewise, how can any dreams or desires God has given us come alive if they're surrounded by fear and squashed by doubt? Things born into captivity cannot flourish. So you and I must strip off the worries and anxieties that have caged us in, one by one, as we realize that in light of God's power, they were never that dangerous to begin with.

Fear is a leaven that can poison the whole batch—our entire faith, our community, and the rest of our years on earth. It's a posture that will weave itself into every area of our lives until we can't remember what it was like to make a decision motivated by faith or hope. Fear will convince us we're playing defense when we were always meant to be on the offense (not offended!) for the kingdom. Fear will cage us and contain us until we're stuck in the confines and constraints that the enemy of our souls has built for us, not running wild and free the way we were created to be. Things born into captivity cannot flourish, and if God is going to grow our desire to run on mission and live abundantly, we've got to allow Him a spacious place in our lives to accomplish it.

Just like in my dream, we become so comfortable around our captors (our fears) that we begin to see them as friends and even comrades—we spend our days with them! We share our lives with them! We straight-up fall prey to Stockholm syndrome. Our fears stop seeming like threats, and eventually we perceive them as helpful boundaries that simplify our lives. In the worst-case scenario, we put spiritual labels on them, maybe even allowing ourselves to believe they were sent by God to help us stay safe. The problem is that we were never meant to stay safe in His kingdom—we were called to go and tell the good news at all costs.

When it comes to sin or lies we believe that hinder us from walking fully with God, I find they're often paired together as double whammies to keep us from obedience. In my life, fear has walked hand in hand with people-pleasing as a tool of torment to keep me in a place I was never meant to be held.

What I mean by this is that for so many of us, one reason fear is so incredibly enticing is because it's culturally accepted and even approved of. Women (and men) who act courageously in obedience, doing what God has called them to do, often create just enough of a stir for them to be publicly praised and privately shunned. We love brave people who listen to the Holy Spirit from afar, but it's not always easy to stand close to them. What if their bold obedience rubs off on us? What if it calls us out of our comfort zones? What if it changes our plans or messes with our preconceived notions of what should be? Brave and courageous followers of God make great leaders, but they're risky to have as friends.

I think this has to do with *muchness*. But let me back up and explain a little.

COME OUT, BIG ALICE

A few years back, my older sister became obsessed with the new rendition of *Alice in Wonderland*, to the point of naming her new twelve-passenger van "Big Alice." I have to admit I giggled at that, but knowing how significant this story had become to her, I decided to give it a watch myself, and one afternoon I hit "play" with my kiddos when they needed some entertaining. The following lines floored me in a big way.

In this scene, Alice has shrunk to an incredibly small size and she's so locked up in fear and doubt that she can't possibly see herself as capable of accomplishing what it's been predicted that she will do. What's more, she can't see the peril everyone else will be in if she refuses to act. This is when the Mad Hatter takes Small Alice aside and says:

You don't slay.
You're not the same as you were before.
You were much more muchier.
You've lost your muchness.

I sat with my mouth open and heard the Holy Spirit loud and clear saying the same thing to me about my current season:

You've gotten small to appease other people.
You've let fear and the approval of humans keep you tidy.

You don't slay; you barely even show up to the battle. You've lost your muchness.

Since that time, if my sister and I catch each other living in fear or playing it small, we'll bellow to one another, "COME OUT, BIG ALICE!" In this way, we remind each other that we're not here to appease other people, and we're not here for their approval. We were placed on this earth by the King of the universe to bring Him glory, to spread His fame, to love His people, to soak up His affection, and to tell our stories. That may be too much for some people, and that will have to be okay.

You know what I realized? There was only one difference between Small Alice and Big Alice: courage.

Isn't it the same for us? By now, you know where we get our courage from. We claim our courage when we believe we are who God says we are.

The phrase "be strong and courageous" is used roughly ten times in the Old Testament, starting in Deuteronomy 31 when Moses is giving some parting words to the Israelites, informing them that Joshua will be his predecessor, but not to worry, because God will go with them:

> Be strong and courageous. Do not be afraid or terrified because of them, for the Lord your God goes with you; he will never leave you nor forsake you. (Deuteronomy 31:6)

In chapter 31 alone, the phrase is used three times. Twice when Moses says it to Joshua and once when God Himself says it to Joshua. Be strong and courageous. In my deep dive into the life of Moses, and thus, into the passing of his ministry to Joshua, I obviously paid serious attention to this phrase that is repeated so deliberately over a few sequential chapters of the Bible. Seven of the ten times the phrase is used are at the at the end of Moses' ministry and the beginning of Joshua's—three times in chapter 1 of the book of Joshua alone.

The Hebrew words always mean the same thing. Here's a quick word study:

Strong in Hebrew essentially just means "strong." No hidden meaning. *Courageous* in Hebrew means just that— courageous. Of good courage. Nothing groundbreaking in this phrase; it's just a command from God to be strong and to be courageous. *Except* when God gets emphatic in Joshua, chapter 1, and changes the language ever so slightly:

"Be strong and *very* courageous." (Joshua 1:7)

Why would I freak out over the word *very*? Why am I leading you down this whole rabbit trail, and what in the world does this have to do with *Alice in Wonderland*?

"Very" in Hebrew is *meod*, which translates to muchness, force, abundance.

Be strong and MUCHNESS courageous, God is telling Joshua here. Be strong and MUCHNESS courageous, women of God. Be strong and MUCHNESS courageous, generation of believers.

Can you imagine for a moment what would have happened if Joshua had refused to step into this calling out of *fear* that he wasn't adequate? Can you imagine if he'd passed on this directive because he just didn't want to ruffle any feathers or because he was worried about stepping into his particularly purposed muchness?

You don't have to imagine what would have happened. The story of Moses, his predecessor, tells us the potential repercussions for such lack of faith. It was doubting God's sovereignty and capacity that led Moses to lose his ability to enter the Promised Land, and it was this exact struggle that put Joshua in position to lead the Israelites into Canaan in Moses' place.

Listening to fear and allowing ourselves to be caged by it has incredible consequences. We see in the story of Moses and Joshua that God's plan is accomplished—He frees His people—but we risk losing opportunity and blessing when we let fear speak louder than our faith.

When we actually begin to fight fear and face it head-on, we will find ourselves slaying it, and not just for our own sakes. We'll be slaying fear left and right, and the victory will always be on the kingdom's side. The Word of God tells us that perfect love casts out fear; that where there's love, there is no room for fear; and that the enemy of our Father and our souls has been defeated (1 John 4:18).

When we gather the weapons we need to demolish the strongholds of fear that set themselves up against the knowledge of God, we will experience freedom and liberty in ways we could never even ask for or imagine, but we might seem like a little . . . *muchness.* We may just have to make a fuss. It may be that we don't seem small anymore, and as we no longer fit in the cages of the enemy, we also will regrettably outgrow the confines within which our culture would prefer to keep us.

Sister-friend, you were made in the image of God—not given a spirit of fear or timidity at birth but born into a spiritual heritage of strength and courage that will at times look like *muchness* to the world. It may seem a little extra. It may ruffle feathers. It may rock the boat. It will absolutely call those around you to evaluate whether or not they're obediently listening to the Father with all they have. But what is the alternative?

We weren't meant to birth kingdom-proclaiming ministries in the midst of captivity. We weren't created to cohabitate with our jailers, to be comforted by the confines of our own doubts and fears. We weren't made to be small; He placed us here to slay. For His glory, and our good, and even for the sake of abundant adventure.

That *muchness* you thought was your liability? Turns out it's your secret weapon.

Come out, Big Alice. You weren't made for fear.

CHAPTER 11

FEAR, FAILURE, AND FIGHTING BACK

What if the circumstances we fear the most are the ones that will afford us the most abundance? What if loss and failure are supposed to be the cornerstones of our testimony? Like Moses, rock bottom is my origin story. But this isn't a sob story, it's my song of victory.

Nick and I got married in 2005. I was twenty, and he was twenty-one, and we're still shaking our heads that our parents let us walk down the aisle. We were 3,045 mistakes waiting to happen all jumbled up together.

Two and a half years later, on little more than a whim and some nudges from the Holy Spirit, we quit our only slightly stable life and moved as far as we possibly could across the United States, from Charlotte, North Carolina, to Seattle, Washington. We had an eleven-month-old, and we were eight months pregnant with another baby.

The next four years were so incredibly painful and difficult, I can barely describe them. We had a third baby when that second baby was just thirteen months old, rounding out our family (temporarily) at three kids under three, three babies born in thirty months. Three C-sections, three recoveries, three bouts of hormones and healing. I was diagnosed with an auto-immune disorder that changed everything about how I saw myself and my capacity to live, love, move, and thrive. I was hit with postpartum depression, not once but twice, until my "bad days" were so severe that suicide felt like another option in my back pocket.

The next few years we dove into ministry as the rest of the country dove into a financial recession. On top of all our other issues, poverty was now our new normal—we searched our car for quarters to buy bananas for breakfast the next morning, and more times than I'd like to remember, we had friends pitch in to pay our bills.

In the midst of all of this, we lost a baby to miscarriage and discovered that medically, all was not right with our children. One of our kids landed in the ICU with catastrophic seizures, and after that hospital stay, our family went through a bout of MRSA infections that we picked up from the hospital. This season was not just hard, it was horrible.

I tried to run an online small business, but I made zero sales. Nick applied at an estimated hundred-plus jobs during those years. We prayed. We cried. Countless other people prayed for us and cried with us.

Maybe it was all our fault. Maybe we made incredibly poor decisions. Maybe it was God's gift to us, and He wanted us to have the grit and grace to move forward with the hard lessons we suddenly had under our belt. Maybe it was spiritual attack, and the enemy of our souls was trying to take us out just a few years into doing life and kingdom work together. Maybe it was a horrific combination of all three?

Whatever it was, it became the most important season of our life to date, and it's the piece of our lives that I most wish others saw: those broken years that bought us our freedom. Here's why:

When you've truly failed and faced defeat head-on, *you're just not as scared anymore.*

I have given all I have to ministry and it has been hard. *I'd still choose to be in ministry.*

I've sought to love people for the sake of the gospel, done it wrong, hurt them and myself, yet *it still seems like a better plan than living for my own comfort.*

I've tried to honor God with my finances, ended up flat broke and destitute, *and found that grace is still free, and the love of God still covers me.*

I've lost people I love, even to the point of death, *and I'm still glad I loved them in the first place.*

I've been an embarrassment, a disappointment, a situation that is hard to look at, *and I've still been seen and furiously loved by God.*

So, here's the thing: I don't think that the way to fight fear is by ignoring it or pretending that whatever we fear could never come to fruition. Instead, when it comes to pressing in where it really matters, past fear and anxiety and all that could go wrong, I think we should walk it all the way out. So what if what we fear most happens? What will that look like? Then we can really decide if it was worth fearing in the first place.

LET'S DIG IN

I went on Instagram a few weeks ago and asked this question: "What is the fear that's keeping you from obedience to His call on your life?" Hundreds and hundreds of replies came in, and I saw the same answers over and over. So let's dive straight into those. You'll notice in the pages to come that my approach to fear is not to excuse it, bury it, or pretend it's not real. Grab your coffee or tea and let's power through these fears in a way that relinquishes their grip on your life.

FAILURE

Out of hundreds of responses from women all over the world, I'm pretty sure every third answer was some version of, "I'm scared to fail." Just as we live, work, and worship in various contexts, I believe this means something different for each person, so let's see if we can pinpoint it a little better. What most women are actually struggling with is one of these three ideas:

> People will see me fail.
> God will see me fail.
> I will know I failed.

People Will See Me Fail:

PEOPLE + FAILURE: I'll never forget the hilarious conversation I had with a friend a few years ago when she called to give me the most heartwarming encouragement that I didn't know I needed. She had seen me hustling hard, working early mornings and late nights, all on ministry-related things. She also saw that

I wasn't working from a place of worship, but rather from a place of worry, so she called to set me free and said, "I want to make sure you know that God will not be disappointed if you fail."

We were on FaceTime, and unfortunately, I'm one of those people who can't hide my emotions, and so as she told me all these endearing things about God not being upset with me, my face went blank. Finally I just giggled a little and said, "God and I are fiiiiiiiine. I'm not worried about God being upset with me if I fail—it's everyone else I'm worried about!"

I hadn't realized it until that moment, but when the walls of my work fell away and the roof came off to reveal what was inside, there it was: all I cared about was making sure other people didn't see me fail. I wasn't even scared of failing in and of itself—I'd failed many times before. I just didn't want to be viewed as a failure.

If you resonate with this, let's walk it all the way out. Let's drag the scary truth into the light and ask two questions: "What if?" and "So what?" What if people see me fail and they are disappointed in me? What if I didn't meet their expectations, and they no longer think I'm important, good, or worthy of being around? What if they tell me I did badly, acknowledge my failure, and equate it to my value as a person? What then? What will happen?

Well, first of all, I won't die. My favorite fictional character, Meredith Grey (*Grey's Anatomy*), the renowned surgeon and all-around tough-woman-who-has-lived-through-it-all, who inspires me and terrifies me all at once, says, "Any day where someone doesn't die is a good day." That's dramatic, and so is *Grey's Anatomy*, but it's still true. Other people seeing you fail will actually not kill you. You'll live to wake up the next day, drink a cup of coffee, and move and breathe and live and go on with your life—at least physically.

What if people see you fail? What else will happen? Well they'll know you're human. They'll know you're just like them, and they'll be given a choice: to pull you closer because they love the idea of being human together, *or* to step away because they wanted you to be infallible. I find that people who push others away when they fail do so because it reminds them of their capacity to make mistakes, and that makes them uncomfortable. So what will *really* happen when people see you fail? *You'll know if they're the kind of people who believe in grace.*

And so what? So what if we lose their approval and affection? If we're being honest, I think we'd rather be in relationship with people who love the grace of God and love dishing it out to others. We'd rather be in close contact with those who take a step toward us when we fail—in love, in grace, just like Jesus.

> When we were utterly helpless, Christ came at just the right time and died for us sinners. (Romans 5:6 NLT)

GOD WILL SEE ME FAIL:

I won't waste my words telling you what will happen when God sees you fail—I'll just tell you His words about it:

> Sin didn't, and doesn't, have a chance in competition with the aggressive forgiveness we call *grace*. When it's sin versus grace, grace wins hands down. All sin can do is threaten us with death, and that's the end of it. Grace,

because God is putting everything together again through the Messiah, invites us into life—a life that goes on and on and on, world without end. (Romans 5:20–21 MSG)

But he said to me, "My grace is sufficient for you, for my power is made perfect in weakness." Therefore I will boast all the more gladly about my weaknesses, so that Christ's power may rest on me. (2 Corinthians 12:9)

Let's end with this one:

For we are His workmanship, created in Christ Jesus for good works, which God prepared beforehand that we should walk in them. (Ephesians 2:10 NKJV)

Sometimes I need the gentle reminder that I can't fail God because He never put me on a pedestal. Not once has God gotten our relationship confused and expected me to be the perfect one. Not once has God put pressure on me to produce something worthy of His affection. Not once in my entire existence has He forgotten that I am the workmanship and He is the creator.

I often forget that, but He never does. So not only does He come in, at just the right time, when I couldn't have chosen Him, but He continually leans in, in His mercy, keeping the roles of our relationship intact. Jesus cannot be disappointed by your failure, because (A) He is all-knowing and chose you anyhow, seeing all your wins and all your losses, and (B) He has never put pressure on you to produce. You are HIS workmanship, and the rest is worship.

Jesus will be your best friend in the midst of your future failures, so we can eliminate disappointing Him from our list of fears.

I WILL SEE ME FAIL:

If we're ready for the people around us to see our potent lack of execution, should we still hide from ourselves? If God Himself is not looking away when we make a mistake, should we be the kind of gals who must bury our heads when the potential for anything less than excellence is on the table?

My answer: only if we want to stay in a place of pride that declares we must be right all the time. This is scary and threatening unless we're humble and understanding our place in the world rightly. Seeing ourselves fail is only something to fear if we've thought for some reason that we're here to make a name for ourselves, rather than declaring we're here to worship, here to love God, and here to help others get connected to His love.

What Is Failure, Anyhow?

Now, let's take a step back toward the work we've already done. In Jesus' name, I believe this is where we're going to find the fuel to blast these fears of failure once and for all.

In part one of this book, we already quit trying to be the best, we acknowledged that our ideal and perfect selves are not our most influential selves, and we took ourselves out of the running to be the hero. In part two, we found that our best motivation for a life of abundant mission is loving others and obsessing over their good. Fearing failure is back to obsessing over *our* good, so there's one more reason we don't have time for that. In part three, we acknowledged that a woman who owns her story, her strengths, and her weaknesses cannot be found out. We were never presenting a picture-perfect persona of ourselves, so we can't fall from the abounding grace in which we already live.

We've spent more time on fear of failure than any of the other fears mainly because it encompasses so many of our apprehensions, but also because I pray that as you apply this process to your own life, your fears will dissipate. I'm praying that as you combat them with truth and give them less power, they will dissolve right before your eyes.

UNQUALIFIED

Did you know Amazon reviews are a *thing* for authors? Maybe some authors pretend they don't read them. Maybe some will tell you their strategies for trying to avoid contact with them, but most of my friends who write books will honestly admit that they *do* read them (even the awful ones) and they develop some kind of coping mechanism to avoid feeling the weight of them.

My game plan for dealing with negative Amazon reviews is something like this:

The first few days a book comes out, I avoid any bad reviews like the plague. Mainly because a scathing and horrific review that comes out the first day or even the first week indicates that this purchaser could *not* have read my book, at least not in its entirety. If they're leaving an Amazon review six hours after the book is published, telling you it's trash, it's probably unlikely that they sat down to read it thoughtfully. This person is what the internet has labeled a "troll." Urban Dictionary defines a troll as "One who posts a deliberately provocative message to a newsgroup or message board with the intention of causing maximum disruption and argument."

I do not feed the trolls. I do not listen to the trolls. We are not on the same team. We do not want the same things. Someone who is on my team, the kingdom team, would not speak about another human being this way—not even their worst enemy.

I wait a few weeks, or a few months if at all possible, and then (girded with prayer and the protection of the Holy Spirit), I read the negative reviews. Every one. Even the horrible troll ones, and I try to just laugh at those. And I hold them all up to the Lord and I say, "Is there anything real you want me to hear from this? In any of these hurtful and hard-to-hear words is there correction or admonition here that I should hold on to?"

I am no longer hiding from these bad reviews, giving them fear-derived power in my life. Instead, I have turned the tables on their potential potency. I am utilizing them for the glory of God, and the enemy can no longer wield them as weapons against me.

The same needs to be true for all our fears, most specifically this one I'm about to address: the lie that there is some benchmark of qualification or readiness in order for you to be used by God. And in case you question for even a moment that you are alone in this fear, I'll tell you two things: it was the second-most-named fear when I asked women what stopped them from walking out what God has called them to do, *and* it is one of my own biggest struggles.

I introduce to you Exhibit A, the Amazon review that almost took me out:

The authors are not spiritually mature enough to lead other women. One is a "pastor's" wife. I use that term loosely.

This review was from my first book, written with my friend Hayley Morgan, and for the longest time, the visual of the word *pastor* in quotation marks just about did me in. The reviewer wasn't just calling me unqualified to write books, she also came after my leadership, and somehow, in one fell swoop, she also attacked the calling of my husband and my fittedness to be his wife.

It's fine, it's fine. IT'S JUST THAT THOSE ARE ALL MY WORST FEARS WRAPPED UP IN ONE SENTENCE!

As I write this, it's a Sunday morning. On Sundays, Nick wakes up at six to sermon prep, and in this season I wake up at five or six to write, so we're facing each other in the living room, me on the camel-colored sofa and him on the gray club chair. He's handwriting the notes for his sermon in his notebook, and I'm tap-tap-tapping away on the keyboard.

Today we'll go to the elementary school where our small church plant meets, and in spite of so much fear, in the midst of a terribly hard season, we'll lead our people into the throne room of grace. We will not do it perfectly. It will not be a pretty or shiny production. But it will be our spiritual act of worship, the one to which God has called us. We are the guy and the girl for the job, even though in this season, it would be so much easier to quit and do something else.

So as I lead you through the fight against this particular fear, I want you to know I am in the trenches with you. I barely graduated from high school, don't remember much from college, and have not been to seminary. I have received a lot of ministry training, but *most* of it has been from doing it wrong and repenting along the way. I feel unqualified with every breath I take, but here is what I know to be true:

> But God chose the foolish things of the world to shame the wise; God chose the weak things of the world to shame the strong. God chose the lowly things of this world and the despised things—and the things that are not—to nullify the things that are, so that no one may boast before him. It is because of him that you are in Christ Jesus, who has become for us wisdom from God—that is, our righteousness, holiness and redemption. (1 Corinthians 1:27–30)

TRUTH #1: God's qualification processes are not like those of humans, even Christians. He chooses the weak, the foolish, the lowly, and the despised. He doesn't leave them that way, but we *must* agree that we can no longer submit to a human standard of qualification to begin with.

In fact, to listen to this lie is to disagree with God and His process of qualification, so let's not do that anymore. Let's not give an ear or another second of our lives to the idea that another human or a group of them gets to decide if we're suitable to be used in the kingdom of God. *Amen?*

TRUTH #2: It is God who does the equipping according to the call. You've heard it before, and it's only a cliché because it's true: He equips who He calls. There is no talent show for Jesus, wherein in the most gifted get the best appointments. The world works that way—often, even the church works that way—but the kingdom of God does not.

Now may the God of peace, who through the blood of the eternal covenant brought back from the dead our Lord Jesus, that great Shepherd of the sheep, equip you with everything good for doing His will, and may He work in us what is pleasing to Him, through Jesus Christ, to whom be glory for ever and ever. Amen. (Hebrews 13:20–21)

TRUTH #3: All the great heroes of the faith that we revere, excluding the perfect son of God, had "disqualifying" characteristics. Someone on Amazon would have used quotations to describe his or her calling at some point, I can promise you that.

Noah got drunk, Paul helped murder Christians, Rahab was a prostitute, Jeremiah and Timothy were too young, Jacob was a liar, Isaiah preached in the nude, the Samaritan woman was a mess, Jonah ran from God, the disciples couldn't stay awake during prayer time, Moses couldn't speak well, David was an adulterer, and Joseph was abused and abandoned.

From all that I know of God, from all that I've seen of the work of Jesus and the power of the Holy Spirit, I never want to be the human standing between God and others, deeming someone unfit. God is the only righteous One, God is the only perfect One, God is the only holy One. If He calls a human being into His service and into His kingdom, you'd better believe that the safest place for me is CHEERING THAT PERSON ON as they obediently answer God's call.

We only touched on the big two fears—fear of failure and the fear that you might not be qualified—but I hope you're catching hold of some wild boldness to fight those accusations and attempts to take you out.

It's not just that we're going to speak the truth to fears, and it's not just that we're going to comfort ourselves in the midst of our fears. Our call is to demolish any idea that sets itself up against the knowledge of God, and fear is just that.

> We demolish arguments and every pretension that sets itself up against the knowledge of God, and we take captive every thought to make it obedient to Christ. (2 Corinthians 10:5)

If you're ready to keep going on this fear-fighting quest, I'll meet you in the next chapter.

CHAPTER 12

GET OUT YOUR MOUSE TRAPS

A few years ago, we had a mice problem.

Don't judge me! It's not a cleanliness issue, I promise. It's a downtown Charleston thing. The whole peninsula of downtown Charleston is about two miles wide by three miles long, and we're surrounded by water on three sides. On this tiny little peninsula are hundreds of restaurants and thousands of tourists and . . . I don't know . . . one million mice? Most of the homes are very old, and the insulation and all other means of mice defense have been weakened by decades of wear on the houses. So in our last house, we had a mice problem.

Our first alert to the situation was alarming. My little sister was babysitting our kids one night when we got a text: "EMERGENCY. THERE IS SOMEONE IN THE KITCHEN." Um, full stop! *What*?! We had an alarm system, and it was set, so we were fairly certain no one had gotten into the house after it was on. We figured one of the kids had snuck into the kitchen. My sister got brave enough to go check and realized there was no human, just definitely some sort of small animal banging around inside the pots and pans. By the time we got home, there was no sign of the mouse.

The telltale signs just kept coming. We'd find our bananas eaten through, cartons of cereal chewed into shreds, even the kids' jackets and shoes were gnawed on in the coat closet. (I want to throw up a little in my mouth remembering this.) They were very loud, sometimes keeping us up at night or waking us up early in the morning with their shenanigans. Over time, it seemed the mice were *taking over*, but here's the crazy part: I never laid eyes on any of the creatures.

I became terrified to be alone downstairs in our home. What if I was having my quiet time one morning and one came out? What would I do?! What if I went to make my coffee in the morning and one skedaddled across my hand?! Would I die right then and there? Maybe. Definitely. *Definitely.*

My life (in my own home) became about avoiding the mice. I lived in extreme and paralyzing fear of hearing them, seeing them, or interacting with them in any way. I constantly bullied my husband into "dealing with them" however he saw fit, but until then, I basically lived on our second floor. For whatever dumb reason, I believed they couldn't or wouldn't climb the stairs. I KNOW, Y'ALL—I WAS IRRATIONAL.

Eventually, we caught one, using the most humane trap possible, of course. We caught it alive (hence the humane) and it woke us up at 3 a.m. with its extreme yelling. Did you know mice yell? They shriek when they're caught! At least, this horrible menace of a mouse did. Nick and I both jumped out of bed, ran down to the kitchen, and prepared to meet this creature who had been torturing us for months. It was time to come face-to-face with this mouse, who had been basically ruining my life and had almost convinced me we needed to move.

We approached slowly, cautiously, trembling (okay, that was just me), and lo and behold, we opened the pantry closet to find the most adorable Disney-character-like cutie patootie of a mouse you've ever seen. It was small and soft and brown, and I swear its large, glassy eyes were looking to us for benevolence and friendship. This was not the four-pound monster rat I'd been picturing stalking my kitchen. I wasn't even sure the little guy had teeth. He was sweet and kind, but still, he had to go—right?

No. In the midst of us trying to transport him out of the trap, he got away. We went to bed at shortly after with the full knowledge that this cute (but precocious) little guy was still somewhere in our house.

But seeing how small and sweet-looking he was? That changed everything for me. I went joyfully downstairs in the morning for my coffee and time with God, no longer scared to see him. Sometimes, if I heard him scurrying around in the cupboards, I'd tell him hello. And he got bolder! We saw him a few times, running across the floor or sneaking into some busted baseboard. Of course, the goal was to catch him, but our little buddy had become so familiar, we didn't go after him with as much gusto.

Until he took it too far.

One night we were hosting a community group in our home, and this was early in our church plant, so it was the only group our church had. There were twenty-five to thirty people scattered all over our living room, some on sofas and some sitting on the floor. Nick was teaching from the Word, and we were getting ready to pray, when out of the corner of my eye, *I saw him*. OUR MOUSE FRIEND WAS COMING OUT. He was moving slowly, approaching the group, and from what I could tell, I was the only one who could see him. I was across the room on the sofa, but there were people sitting on the floor, and he was getting closer to them.

Friends, I want you to know that what I'm about to say is not even slightly fabricated or exaggerated. That crazy mouse scampered all the way into the middle of our group of friends and plopped down. I was dying. No one saw him but me. Until they did.

It all happened so fast, I can't remember if I gasped or if someone saw him and screamed, but everything became chaotic very quickly. In the wake of the screams, he ran away, and we tried to continue the group, but there was no going back. A MOUSE HAD JUST JOINED US. And I was terrified all of those people were going to go home and find a new church.

And that is when our gentle acceptance of the mice ended.

I will spare you the rest of the details, but a few months later our house was more tightly secured than a government building. Any and all mice were eradicated, and we never saw another one again.

STOP PLAYING NICE

A few months later, the Holy Spirit showed me that I treat my fears like I treated my mice. I either gave them way too much power and changed my life because of them *or* I let them live peacefully around me, growing too comfortable with their presence.

But we were never meant to play nice with our fears—since God is love and light, and in Him there is no darkness at all, we must fight any ideas that challenge the truth that He is good, He loves us, and we can trust Him. That is what fears are: enemies of God's love and our belief in it. Second Corinthians tells us exactly what to do with these thoughts, in no uncertain terms:

> We demolish arguments and every pretension that sets itself up against the knowledge of God, and we take captive every thought to make it obedient to Christ. (v. 10:5)

We looked at this passage at the end of the previous chapter. It's one that the Lord used to show me I can't play nice with *any* idea that comes between me and my worship of Him. And every fear is just that: an argument against God's goodness, His provision, His holiness, His worthiness, and His faithfulness in my life.

Instead of utilizing the truth found in the Word of God and the power of the Holy Spirit that I've been given to fight spiritually, I have the propensity to treat my fears like a three-inch mouse that is freaking me out, locking me up, and keeping me from using what I've got. Or worse, I get so used to my fears, I stop realizing how much of a pest they are to have around. I grow complacent in my pursuit to eradicate them from my life, inviting them to stay, making room for them, and forgetting they were never meant to live in my house.

We went for the two biggest fears most of us are struggling

with in the last chapter: the fear of failure and the fear that we're inadequate. For most of us, these are monumental, and tipping over those strongholds is no easy task. It may have been the first time you actually faced those fears and realized how unhealthy they are; it may have been the first time you realized you *could* do battle against them. And I want to respect that, for the majority of us, those two fears are colossal. They're not bigger than God. They're not stronger the Spirit. But they take work to overcome.

I want to invite you into a different scenario with our next few fears. I want you to feel armed with the wild hope of what a life might look like when it no longer answers to fear. I want you to imagine, maybe for the first time, how it might feel to make decisions based on calling and purpose, rather than what's comfortable, attainable, or risk-free.

Mostly, I want you to proceed as if some very stupid small pests are running around your spiritual house, and *you have had enough.* Let's put the following fears in their place, realizing they are much smaller and less powerful than we are. Let's kick them out of our thought lives, our work lives, our family relationships, our friendships, our callings—*forever.* You in? Let's go.

YOU GUYS GOT TO GO

For Those Who Are Scared They Heard God Wrong:

Was I really supposed to start this ministry?
Did I hear God wrong about marrying this person?
Was having kids my idea or His idea?

Did I just imagine that call in my heart to go back to grad
school?
Did I somehow make a colossal mistake that took my
whole life off His path?

"Did God really say this?" Many of us are walking around
with this thought rattling around in our heads, and I can't get
past how much the enemy must be giggling over it. This makes
me mad and compels me to pull out some serious traps for this
lie. If this question has repeatedly plagued you, I'm going to
hand you a series of weapons to come hard against this pit into
which the enemy of your soul wants to lure you.

When you wonder if you really heard God correctly,
whether it's about a calling, a decision, or a life choice, when
you wonder if you can step out in faith, not knowing if He'll
be there to back you up; when you wonder if you've gotten too
big for your britches and you might be ahead of God, *remind
yourself of the following:*

Knowing exactly what God wants us to do is not the aim of
our life; worship is. There is so much mighty truth in the Word
of God about willfully going against His will and His ways,
but there are no verses denouncing us for trying to honor and
please Him and accidentally making a misstep.

God has never said that if we hear Him wrong, we're
out. He's never said He'll leave us if we misinterpret what we
thought He had planned for our lives.

I, the LORD, have called you in righteousness;
I will take hold of your hand.
I will keep you and will make you

> to be a covenant for the people
> and a light for the Gentiles,
> to open eyes that are blind,
> to free captives from prison
> and to release from the dungeon those who sit
> in darkness. (Isaiah 42:6–7)

The LORD himself goes before you and will be with you; he will never leave you nor forsake you. Do not be afraid; do not be discouraged. (Deuteronomy 31:8)

I am 100 percent sure that you will misinterpret something about God at some point. You'll read a Bible verse out of context or think He was pointing you in some direction that He wasn't. But misinterpreting and willfully disobeying God are two wildly different things. More than that, the truth of our reality is that we're held in God's kingdom by grace—not by our flawless interpretation, perfect attendance, or impeccable obedience.

We no longer live under the power of the fear of failure, so let's say we hear God wrong and massively fall flat on our faces. So what? Has God left us? No.

Here's an even better tool in your toolbox regarding this fear: let's say another person has called into question your ability to hear from God. Your husband doubts this idea you have, your best friend doubts your capacity to start a new ministry, or your parents feel dubious about where you want to go to college.

This is one of the enemy's favorite tools to isolate us and make us run from God. The cycle looks something like this: We think we hear from God. Our people doubt us. We respond in frustration, hurt, pride, and extreme offense when they express that. Inside, we doubt that we hear from God too, so we're having a mini crisis of faith while outwardly defending ourselves. If the thing we thought we heard from God works out well, we're still prideful and now maybe indignant, telling the people in our life we told them so. If it doesn't go well according to the world's standards, they may become prideful and triumphant and push us away. Either way, the doubt gets louder, and the refreshing power of community gets watered down.

If you read this just now and got angry all over again at someone who has been a part of that cycle in your life, I'd like to encourage you to pause. Know this: Satan is the enemy. Fear is the enemy. Anything that sets itself up against the knowledge of God is the enemy. Not your friend/spouse/parent/coworker/sibling/child/grandparent. We've all played a part in broken cycles, but there is a new way.

What if you said this to them:

You doubt whether or not I hear from God correctly? What a coincidence! Me too! Will you pray with me for discernment? Will you remind me that God still loves me if I make the wrong decisions? Will you ask me good questions to help me make wise decisions if I promise to thoughtfully think through them with humility?

I appreciate that you love me enough to bring this into the light for me. I'm so relieved that neither of us needs to feel the pressure to understand every move and thought of God. I'm going to seek God's Word and make sure this thing I'm hearing is consistent with His character and counsel—will you help me? And will you stick around if I do it wrong? I'm earnestly trying not to, but I know it might come to that.

What if we just took all the power and all the weapons

away from the enemy before we got started? He wants to plague us with doubt, but we're not scared of doubt. He wants to separate us from other humans, so we draw closer. He wants to set us up for feeling abandoned by God, so we acknowledge that our Father isn't going anywhere.

I get that you're afraid you might hear God incorrectly. You might. You have. And you will. It doesn't mean He's broken; it means you're human. It doesn't freak Him out, and it doesn't have to freak you out. He's not going anywhere, and you're not going to let this break your whole life. This is a tiny little mouse, and it's time to remove it from the premises. Amen?

For Those Worried about Losing Their Comfort:

This might be a strange thing to say, but can I just acknowledge how blessed I am that you're concerned about this? Because, in the name of Jesus, I pray you *do* lose your comfort.

God's Word speaks to a massive loss of comfort when we follow Him faithfully and obediently. Let's take a look:

> Then Jesus told his disciples, "If anyone would come after me, let him deny himself and take up his cross and follow me. For whoever would save his life will lose it, but whoever loses his life for my sake will find it. For what will it profit a man if he gains the whole world and forfeits his soul? Or what shall a man give in return for his soul? (Matthew 16:24–26 ESV)

The Bible almost promises a loss of comfort to those who follow a kingdom path, but this is a great time to shake our heads and ask: Is that really what we wanted, anyhow? Did we want to get to the end and say, *Well, at least I was comfortable?* I feel like we know enough about one another at this point to know the answer is no. At the very core of who we are, because we're made in the image of Christ, we want what He wants. We want our lives wrung out for the glory of God. We want to make an impact. We want more people to know Him. *We* want to know more of Him.

But this bad news (that your fear is real) comes with a heavy dose of good news: where kingdom living promises to strip away your earthly comfort, supernatural joy and at-ease-ness is your birthright.

> The LORD is my shepherd, I lack nothing.
>> He makes me lie down in green pastures,
> He leads me beside quiet waters,
>> he refreshes my soul.
> He guides me along the right paths
>> for his name's sake.
> Even though I walk
>> through the darkest valley,
> I will fear no evil,
>> for you are with me;
> Your rod and your staff,
>> they comfort me. (Psalm 23:1–4)

The world makes promises it just can't keep: take care of yourself, work hard, do what you love, surround yourself with amazing things, and you'll find comfort. And yet *life happens.* Life is full of discomfort: twists, turns, pain, processes, growth, heartache, and death. It just *is!* These things aren't God's fault;

they are the natural design of a world still experiencing the ache of the fall, the broken covenant that dates back to the Garden of Eden. This is what life is like when we are separated from God corporately: *uncomfortable.*

And yet, there is a balm for our souls in the midst of it all: spiritual, everlasting comfort can be ours by the power of the Holy Spirit, by the intercession purchased with the blood of Jesus. His presence, His power, His friendship are all ours to access because our Savior purchased our place in the throne room of grace.

It may be guaranteed that a life lived for the glory of God will cost our comfort, but it's an eternal promise that we'll have *Him* as our comfort. He will be our peace.

For Those Who Fear Rejection:

I pray this chapter is an encouragement instead of a massive downer as I let you in on the secret that most of our greatest fears in life are real concerns that the Word of God confirms *will* happen.

Yes, you will be rejected.

Let's rephrase that. You *most definitely will* be rejected.

At some point in your life, you are going to come up against rejection. Someone (or many someones) will take a long hard look at you and decide: *I don't like her. She's not for me.*

It may be because you're too spiritual. It may be because you're too kind. It may be because you're too pretty or too ugly in their eyes. Perhaps you are too smart, or maybe it's because you weren't educated properly. You might have said too much or said too little. You might be rejected because you did something wildly wrong or because you refused to cosign on their sin. It's likely that at some point, you'll be rejected because you actually did something awful or had bad intentions, and they refused to give you grace. There's also the potential for you to be rejected when you did absolutely nothing wrong. You're in good company, because this is also Jesus' story.

Here's a prophecy spoken about Him thousands of years before His birth:

> He had no beauty or majesty to attract us to Him, nothing in His appearance that we should desire Him. He was despised and rejected by mankind, a man of suffering, and familiar with pain. Like one from whom people hide their faces He was despised, and we held Him in low esteem. Surely He took up our pain and bore our suffering, yet we considered him punished by God, stricken by him, and afflicted. But He was pierced for our transgressions, He was crushed for our iniquities; the punishment that brought us peace was on Him, and by His wounds we are healed. (Isaiah 53:2–5)

Later on, Jesus Himself would speak about His rejection *and* our not-so-potential rejection as well:

> If the world hates you, keep in mind that it hated me first. If you belonged to the world, it would love you as its own. As it is, you do not belong to the world, but I have chosen you out of the world. That is why the world hates you. (John 15:18–19)

At the end of the day, this one isn't really worth fearing, because it *is* going to happen. We *are* going to be rejected. We just get to decide how we're going to respond and if we're going to spend our whole lives trying to avoid something that's inevitable.

Jesus' response to rejection was compassion, love, and moving on. He never yelled, "OH YEAH! YOU DON'T LIKE ME?" at followers who turned away from Him; instead, He had compassion on them. My favorite example of this is in Luke 19, when Jesus is coming to Jerusalem to give His life for us, and is still in the thick of experiencing rejection. He can see it all, hold it all, the whole history of humanity, and He can somehow experience people waving palm branches at Him in worship, knowing these same people will shout in favor of His crucifixion just days later.

In Luke 19, He stops and weeps at the city gates, broken over what their rejection means for *their* future, not just His.

Before His death, as He was instructing the disciples how to go out and share the good news, He gave this prescriptive advice on how to handle rejection: "If anyone will not welcome you or listen to your words, leave that home or town and shake the dust off your feet" (Matthew 10:14).

The answer isn't just found in acknowledging that rejection is headed our way, but also in throwing it off. To me, it seems the healthiest way to handle rejection is as follows:

a. Feel it. It's painful. Don't stuff it or pretend it doesn't exist. Ask God to comfort you. If you've actually done something wrong and you've been rejected for a good reason, repent! Tell God you're sorry, and people too if that's applicable, and ask Him to change your heart.

b. Stay soft toward those who rejected you. This one is harder. Don't treat them like monsters, and don't start believing that God doesn't love them or want good for them. As much as you can, at least in your heart, be on their team. Ask Him to help you want good for them, even if from afar. Ask Him to help you see the best in them, even when you're probably seeing the worst.

c. Move on! Shake it off. Keep going. Don't spite them and say, "Forget you!" but do move on and stop trying to seek their approval. For whatever reason, you didn't get it, and you've got more kingdom work to do. Keep going.

Rinse and repeat. *One million times.*

The bad news is that your fear is real—rejection is on the way. The good news is that Jesus has the comfort and answer that you need. You're in good company, and you weren't put here on earth to win a popularity contest, anyway.

The world around you is hurting, dying, and in pain. God is the hero, and you are the rescue plan. This life is not about the approval of others, and rejection *is* going to come. Let's be women who are prepared for it, who expect it, even, but who handle it with health, grace, and maturity.

For Those Who Fear It Will Be about Them:

"I'm worried I'm going to make this whole thing about me."

"I'm worried I'll do what I want to do, not what God asks me to do."

"I'm worried I'll be seeking my fame and not God's."

Slap a smile on your face; this is happy, I promise.

Because the answer is the same here, but I swear it's still good news.

You will! You absolutely *will* make it about you. All the time. Over and over again.

You'll do something "for God" and feel proud of yourself on the inside. You'll do something in His name that is exactly what you wanted to do. You'll take credit for something that was amazing and incredible, but which He actually did all on His own. You *will* make it about you.

And He will give you grace—the way He always does. And His grace will compel you to try again, for His glory, once again. I trust you will make it about you because you are human, the same way I am sure I will make it about me because I am human, too.

But I also trust that the Holy Spirit will work in and through you, making you feel twisty or bummed out at some point (this is what we call *conviction*), because you weren't made to glorify you.

I love it when women confess this worry to me as a legitimate fear, because the fact that it's a fear at all confirms that you *want* His name to be made famous more than you want yours to be glorified. That fear shows you have a healthy and beautiful desire for glory.

What about all the people out there who are making it about themselves? Why isn't God convicting *them*? I don't know. Maybe He is. Maybe I can't see the whole picture. Maybe He just hasn't convicted them yet but will. It's not my business, though, and I can't control it.

What I can (sort of) control is my own heart. I can bet all I've got that I will make serving God and His people, following His call, and living for His name and kingdom about me at many points in my life. But I'm also willing to bet with all that I've got that God will use it anyhow.

WHAT WE KNOW SO FAR

Some of our fears are irrational, and some are just real-life eventualities coming our way. But we can't let them be king and let Jesus be King at the same time. There is so little we have control over—what will happen to us, what people will do, what will happen in life—but we do have the ever-present option to love God and love His people.

And perfect love casts out fear.

Let's be women of love, not limited by what *might* come our way. Let's be women defined by action and activated faith, trusting God and His Word over how things look, how we feel, or what we fear.

You are the girl for the job. You are the one placed right where you're at, on purpose, to live for His glory and to resist the scary things. You were made to worship through fear. You were made to see Him and His hand as bigger than anything headed your way. These are tiny little mice of fear, and we were meant to catch them, eradicate them, and help other women clean out their houses, too. So go ahead—get your traps out, and let's take care of these fears for good.

CATCH THE VISION

Because God is a generous communicator
and friend, and He is on your side.

CHAPTER 13

THE STAGE WE CRAVE (AND SOMETHING BETTER)

I've got one kiddo who will remain nameless for the following story. For the record, I did ask permission to share this, but I've decided that they aren't old enough to *truly* consent, so we're keeping it anonymous.

This sweet kiddo of mine is a dreamer. And I love it.

One day this past summer, said kiddo watched their first episode of *America's Got Talent*. *America's Got Talent*, or *AGT* for short, is a reality-TV show that's also a talent competition, and my kids were hooked *quick*. After a few episodes, this one child cuddled up to me on the sofa and said they wanted to have a serious conversation. I put down what I was doing, turned to face them, and gave them my full attention.

ANONYMOUS CHILD: "I would like to try out for *America's Got Talent*."

ME: "Um. Ok. For what talent?"

ANONYMOUS CHILD: (looking shocked and offended) "Are you serious? Singing, of course."

ME: "You like to sing? I mean, I've honestly never heard you sing. I'm just a little surprised, because you've never been in a choir or even had a singing lesson."

ANONYMOUS CHILD: "Right. I'm just naturally talented. And I'd like to go on *America's Got Talent*."

ME: (flabbergasted) "Okay. Okay. Well, um . . . why don't we start with singing lessons and see how you are at singing?"

ANONYMOUS CHILD: (stone-cold serious) "I'll agree to go to singing lessons once if you'll listen when they tell you that I don't really need lessons and I'm ready for *America's Got Talent*."

ME: (flabbergasted) "I really wish I had your confidence and vision for life."

What followed was *weeks* of conversation, weeks of being harassed by this incredibly headstrong kid of mine, who was absolutely and irrevocably dedicated to the vision they had for their life: singing onstage at *America's Got Talent*. And while there was a huge part of me that was impressed and blessed by their tenacity, I knew that they had the wrong vision to get started.

This kiddo didn't see the practice it would take to become great at singing. They didn't see the correction and the learning that would give them a solid foundation in music. My sweet child couldn't grasp a picture of the dedication or determination it would take to go to audition after audition and hear no after no.

They weren't considering the ways this gift of singing could be used to help or serve anyone else. They also weren't considering the joy that could come *just* from singing—not from performing or receiving approval from others.

All they could see was the stage. And sometimes, all we can see is the stage, too. We often start with a vision that is all about our glory, comfort, and joy, and by doing so, we miss out on the very best parts of being women who are used by God to change the world.

Now, my kiddo is just that—a kid! So they get a pass at seeing the world this way for a little longer. But we, women of God, know better, and therefore, we can do better. Let's deconstruct the vision of the stage so we can step into a vision much richer—a vision cast by God. Let's peel back the cover and see what ambitions are sitting in our hearts, and let's trade them for a desire to serve and see abundance, so we won't miss out on the best parts of life, love, mission, and ministry.

SHADOWS, NOT THE STAGE

The first time I showed Nick the outline for this book, he gave me such great feedback, and I took it to heart. He looked through every chapter proposal, the grand scheme of all the steps to live on mission, and said, "I think you're missing one thing. There needs to be a section on what happens when it doesn't go well, gets hard, or doesn't look how they thought it would."

The more I thought about his suggestions, the more I agreed. So I want to go for it right now, as we're talking about vision for our lives. Before we ask God to point us in a direction or fortify our hearts for the vision toward which we're already headed, let's see what's behind the stage. Let's pull back the curtain and take a good, hard look at the dark shadows behind our highest hopes.

If I'm honest, where it matters most in my life, I am in a shadow season. And I feel like God is asking me to be honest about that—about what it looks like and how it impacts the vision I had for my life.

If the stage is where most people begin casting vision for their life, and backstage is the reality that most of us live in, I'd say Nick and I are currently ducking in the shadows of the backstage, sitting in the dust to gather some strength, and we're praying. When it comes to church planting, we're tired and discouraged. We've seriously considered quitting. As leaders, we've been put through the ringer. We've lived a lot of stress in the past few months with very little fruit. We've stopped saying, "This is as hard as it gets!" because inevitably, something will happen that makes life and ministry even harder later.

Two days ago, Nick went on a prayer walk, to seek God's face and heart and hopefully find some encouragement, and he came back more discouraged than ever. We sat in the gray club chairs by our front windows, and I was silent, watching his lip quiver. I prayed loudly inside my head, scared to make the wrong move or say the wrong thing. Did he need sympathy? Did he need admonishment? Did he need Scripture?

This, my friends, is not the stage. When your husband is so discouraged and beaten down by a life of mission that he can't articulate what he needs, this is not the stage. When you've been through the ringer with him and your confidence and faith is so wrecked that you're out of words, this is not the stage.

We sat in silence, me scared to say anything out of fear that my doubt and discouragement would leak all over Nick. He was being cautious not to say too much and pull me into his despair. So we just sat.

I told him he could quit if he needed to. But I also told him I didn't think that was what God wanted. And then I prayed for him and went to run an errand.

I dropped off one of our kids at a playdate, and as I drove back, the Holy Spirit rose up in me and showed me a vision: not of the stage, not of how easy it would be if we quit, but of the immeasurable amount of despair we'd feel if we slunk away, sulking as we went.

For whatever reason, I thought about *Grey's Anatomy* and the medical scenarios I've seen depicted on that incredible show. If it's medically inaccurate, please don't tell me—it will totally ruin this analogy for me.

Twice, many seasons apart, there has been a scenario on *Grey's Anatomy* wherein someone has appeared to be dead but is really just frozen. Their heart has stopped beating and they're no longer breathing, but it's because their body temperature has dropped dramatically. Both times, the team attending to them has continued to hope that the person will wake up once their body temperature is normal again. Both times they've used the line, "She's not dead till she's *warm* and dead." They won't pronounce the patient deceased until their body temperature has risen and they still can't be resuscitated. And both times, wouldn't you know, once the patient's body temperature rose, their heart started beating, their brain functions returned, and they made a full recovery.

I repeat: do not tell me if this is not a real, feasible scenario. I'm okay with people fact-checking my theology, but never my *Grey's Anatomy*, you know?

Anyhow, on this discouraging Thursday, God reminded me of that story. *She's not dead till she's warm and dead.* And for whatever reason, that was wildly comforting to me. There may be a day when God calls us to lay down church planting altogether, even though I don't foresee it. But it won't be because we don't have enough volunteers for the nursery. It won't be because the tithe has been a little low for a few months. And it won't be because a few people who don't believe that going to church is all that valuable anymore have left. Those are just temporary symptoms, and they are not enough to make us pack it in forever. If we quit, it will be because God Himself told us that we're done, and that this particular season of ministry is over.

I walked back in from dropping off our son and marched up to our bedroom.

"I've got a message for you, Nick Connolly," I said. "We're not going out like this! Maybe leading a church is not pretty or shiny right now, but God has not told us to quit. It's time to keep going, and you can feel discouraged, you can take a break, you can do whatever you need to do—but we're not quitting."

His slight smile told me that the Holy Spirit had been ministering to Him while I was gone, and he said, "I'm already feeling better, too."

This is not the stage ministry of our church, and I'm starting to believe that it's God's grace to me and to you that I'm writing from the shadows of a hard season.

In the shadows, you know it's all about His power and presence. In the shadows, you remember why you started. In the shadows, you don't feel the warmth and affection of the crowd staring back at you, but you *do* feel the grit and the glory of a God who uses broken people to tell a beautiful story. After the shadows have passed, you will feel the pulse of new life beating into the once dark places. I'm believing that for me, and for you as well.

DON'T TAKE MY WORD FOR IT

Rejoice in the Lord always. I will say it again: Rejoice! Let your gentleness be evident to all. The Lord is near. Do not be anxious about anything, but in every situation, by prayer and petition, with thanksgiving, present your requests to God. And the peace of God, which transcends all understanding, will guard your hearts and your minds in Christ Jesus. (Philippians 4:4–7)

The Apostle Paul is believed to have written 28 percent of the New Testament, four of those books being letters written from jail. Talk about a vision for ministry that wasn't centered around the stage! One of these letters was written to the church in Philippi, a church Paul helped to plant on his second missionary journey. One major theme of the letter to the Philippians is joy, with gratefulness being a second theme.

If God is the hero and we are the rescue plan, and if we're on the same page—that we're doing all of this for His glory and His fame—there is one important piece of the vision we must always factor in. Before we begin to picture where He wants us to go, before we partner with the Holy Spirit to develop any future perception about what He has in store for us, we need to keep one incredibly important character in our viewpoint.

Him.

He's the goal, He's the prize, He's the author and perfecter of our faith and our mission. He's the One who started this whole shebang, and He'll be the One who works it out. He brings the peace, and He brings the power.

I highly suggest that you when you develop a vision for your life, you don't start with a picture of yourself on the stage, whatever that looks like for you. Throw out the images of you winning, excelling, or holding the trophy—only you will know what those pictures look like. My personal encouragement in this season: *anticipate the shadows*. Don't fear them or hide from them; don't worry about what you'll do when they come. Don't avoid them, either, because His light shines in our darkness, too.

But when you anticipate the shadows, remember that the Lord has not left you. The Spirit of God will still be working in and through you, for His glory and YOUR good. His capacity + your obedience = abundance, even on dark Thursdays.

CHAPTER 14

CATCH THE VISION

So we've given up on being the best; we've said goodbye to our ideal selves. God gave us a *who*; He reminded us of the people we're meant to serve, and we made it all about them. We took an honest look at where we've been and the tools He has given us to use for His glory and the good of others. He helped us fight fear, so we can press through and take our place in the kingdom with fervor. And now . . . this is our moment to ask Him, *Where do you want us to go, and what is it that you want us to do?* We need some vision.

I'd love to tell you about my vision. About the picture that keeps me going.

The secret is out now, it just took the majority of the book for me to say it clearly: I'm telling you that you are the girl for the job during the season when I most feel like quitting. I believe God planned it so that I'd need to believe this message for myself at the exact same time that my fingers would be typing the words for you. And like all good, weak seasons, I pray it has strengthened the veracity of the report. These aren't words I'm spouting from a stage; rather, this is a declaration I'm penning from the shadows. I need the words, His Word, and the kingdom narrative to be true more than I ever have before.

While our actual story is hard to share, since it involves our church and other real, live people with different perspectives, I can tell you that there was a peak in the pain, a week that brought some of our biggest fears to the surface. There were then three or four nights of meetings one week that left us just racked, confused, and broken over what was happening around us and to us. At the end of one meeting, I dropped to my knees and just broke. I didn't know when I would stop crying, and I remember thinking, *I don't know if the church will come back from this, and I'm not sure that we will as leaders.*

Hindsight, man. It's a helpful tool. That was a little over three months ago, and I know now that while that night was incredibly painful, it was only the warm-up for the pressure the following days would bring. I also believe that God was using that night as another refinement process, a growing lesson, and I believe we'll likely experience harder days to come in our ministry. Hindsight also gives me compassion for that girl (me), for the fight she was in—the fight for belief and joy in the midst of confusion and hurt.

Something that developed almost immediately during those rough days was an intense fear regarding attending our church. Forget leading or teaching or even making the announcements, I was terrified just to set foot in the place. I know that women across America who have struggled with church hurt at the hand of broken leaders know what I'm talking about, but I've also come face-to-face with church hurt that flows the other way. Leaders sometimes get pummeled and punished by church members, and it's not always easy to know how to handle that. I was a leader who'd gotten bruised in some serious church hurt, and I was scared to go back. Nick, as my pastor and husband, was constantly letting me off the hook and telling me it was absolutely okay if I needed a break. But that felt like quitting and hiding, and that wasn't what God had called me to, so I began to mentally prepare for returning the following Sunday.

I thought through Scriptures I could memorize, breath prayers I could pray when faced with messy feelings, and even motivations to focus on, but the Holy Spirit came in quick and hot with a better solution than I could ever have mustered up for myself. My Father, by the miraculous power of the Holy Spirit, gave me a vision to hold on to when I needed it most.

A few nights before I'd need to go back to church, when I was in the midst of the most pain, without me praying for it or asking Him to, God gave me a dream that still brings an involuntary smile to my face.

Now, I'll often ask God for a dream in a dark season. I'll pray for vision, or I'll just say, "Meet me while I sleep tonight?" But that wasn't the case on this night. In fact, I fell asleep holding my phone, while watching *The West Wing*. And sometime in the hours before I woke, this is what I dreamed:

I was at Bright City, our church, and it was the very next Sunday—the Sunday I was dreading. We were doing all the little, last-minute things needed to get the service started, and I was handling all the small issues and details. In the midst of the dream, with every logistical element I had to problem-solve, it was as if God would pause the dream and show me something.

He would show me a problem that was still going to be an issue, He would show me a person who was not going to leave.

In the dream, He'd let me hear snippets of conversations to inform me about the good that was on the way for the church.

In real life (not in the dream), we'd recently taken out our third column of chairs because we'd had such a large dip in attendance, but we were also feeling a Spirit-led tug to add another service. Typically, in church world, you don't add another service unless you're bursting at the seams, but our pastor (my husband) had this God-sized dream in his heart to start one more service, on a different day. God had given Nick a vision for a Monday night service, where people who might not feel comfortable in church on a Sunday or who might not be able to attend church on a Sunday could come.

In the dream, God showed me we would have to quickly add back in more seats. Then, not only did those seats fill up, but suddenly another space developed in the room next to us, and I saw us running back and forth in between the two places, exhausted but so happy to be obedient.

And then, near the end of the dream, I started seeing different people groups filing in to our church—specific people groups who don't currently attend our church and may not feel comfortable attending any church in our city—and as they walked in, smiling, they'd say, "We're so glad you invited us!" and I'd say, "We're so glad you're here!" The dream ended just as I was giving up my seat so they could all sit down.

I woke up in the early morning with intense feelings of shock and awe.

Then, I heard the Lord say *Luke 14*, as clear as a bell in my head and in my heart.

I grabbed my phone from beside my pillow (I know it's a bad habit; I had fallen asleep watching *The West Wing*, remember?)

and googled Luke 14, too groggy to remember what happened in that portion of the Bible.

> Jesus replied: "A certain man was preparing a great banquet and invited many guests. At the time of the banquet he sent his servant to tell those who had been invited, 'Come, for everything is now ready.'
>
> "But they all alike began to make excuses. The first said, 'I have just bought a field, and I must go and see it. Please excuse me.'
>
> "Another said, 'I have just bought five yoke of oxen, and I'm on my way to try them out. Please excuse me.'
>
> "Still another said, 'I just got married, so I can't come.'
>
> "The servant came back and reported this to his master. Then the owner of the house became angry and ordered his servant, 'Go out quickly into the streets and alleys of the town and bring in the poor, the crippled, the blind and the lame.'
>
> "'Sir,' the servant said, 'what you ordered has been done, but there is still room.'
>
> "Then the master told his servant, 'Go out to the roads and country lanes and compel them to come in, so that my house will be full. I tell you, not one of those who were invited will get a taste of my banquet.'" (Luke 14:16–24)

The next Sunday at church wasn't miraculous. Homeless people didn't come in off the street and get saved, and I don't remember any of the people groups I'd seen in my dream. To be completely honest, some of the people God showed me would stay have left since then. I don't know if He was showing me a prophetic, see-the-future type of dream or if He was just showing me that I didn't have to be scared. But I know that the dream reminded me of my *who*, my *why*.

Those are a few things I think He could have been doing or saying through the dream, but here's the big one: I believe God was reminding me that He is alive, active, and wildly involved in my life. It seemed like He was saying to me, *I'm listening! I'm here! I'm a part of this story, too.*

And for that, I am incredibly grateful. If He's in, if He's here, I'm down for whatever comes my way. Catching a vision does so many incredible things for us—it connects us to the heart of God, it reminds us that this was His plan, and it helps us press in during heartbreakingly hard seasons. We are women who need vision, and we know a Savior who is incredibly willing to share.

TRY IT. YOU'LL LIKE IT

We're rapidly approaching the point of diminishing returns. There's a line we can cross where I do too much talking regarding allowing God to give you a vision for your life, and it begins to eat into the actual time you need to just be with Him to catch said vision. But before you go, here is my earnest plea for you:

Try it. You'll like it.

How do I know God wants to give you a vision for your life? How do I know He wants to have an active, present part in what happens in your world? Here are a few passages of Scripture:

Whether you turn to the right or to the left, your ears will hear a voice behind you, saying, "This is the way; walk in it." (Isaiah 30:21)

All this I have spoken while still with you. But the Advocate, the Holy Spirit, whom the Father will send in my name, will teach you all things and will remind you of everything I have said to you. Peace I leave with you; my peace I give you. I do not give to you as the world gives. Do not let your hearts be troubled and do not be afraid. (John 14:25–27)

I have much more to say to you, more than you can now bear. But when he, the Spirit of truth, comes, he will guide you into all the truth. He will not speak on his own; he will speak only what he hears, and he will tell you what is yet to come. He will glorify me because it is from me that he will receive what he will make known to you. All that belongs to the Father is mine. That is why I said the Spirit will receive from me what he will make known to you. (John 16:12–15)

If any of you lacks wisdom, you should ask God, who gives generously to all without finding fault, and it will be given to you. But when you ask, you must believe and not doubt, because the one who doubts is like a wave of the sea, blown and tossed by the wind. That person should not expect to receive anything from the Lord. Such a person is double-minded and unstable in all they do. (James 1:5–8)

Now I'll make my case for what I believe Scripture promises us.

Jesus was sent that we might have reconciliation with God, our Father. He paid the price for our transgressions and defeated death and sin when He rose from the dead, forever stepping in as the substitute so we can have a relationship with God.

But that relationship doesn't have to be only for eternity in heaven because of the Holy Spirit, the third part of the wild and beautiful nature of our triune God that works on our behalf here on earth, even when Jesus isn't physically here. The Spirit is God made accessible to us, in our hearts, in our homes, in our words and minds. And Jesus was constantly telling us how it would be *better* for us when the Holy Spirit came—how the Holy Spirit would give us guidance, wisdom, comfort, peace, and company.

And I believe with all I've got that there is no reason the Holy Spirit would want to withhold all that from you.

I believe what God's Word says: if you ask for wisdom, you'll get it.

I believe our Father delights in giving good gifts, and one of the best gifts He gives is light for our path, especially when we're asking in earnest so we can give Him more glory.

Do I think He always gives it in a dream? No.

Do I think He always tells us every single little step? It hasn't happened that way for me.

But do I think there's any reason He'd hold back from you? No.

With all I've got, I believe that as much as you want God, *He wants to give you Himself even more.* The Word tells me that the blood of Jesus has purchased our place in the throne room of grace, and it's our birthright as children of God to walk in boldly and ask what He's promised.

Are you ready to ask Him for some vision now?

(Oh my word, I'm so excited. It's about to get good.)

HOW, YOU ASK?

I've never been so expectant for a chapter to end, because to be honest, I cannot imagine the fruit that is about to pour out when the women of God shut this book and head to private places with God to ask for vision, some of you for the millionth time ever and some of you for the absolute first time. Whether it's your first or your 5,501st time, here are some quick thoughts from me to you about asking God to get loud and clear with you.

1. It's not weird, it's biblical.

I have a bad habit of calling things "weird" that God has called good. I used to call my body weird and I used to call our church weird, and one day a sweet college-age boy walked up to me at church and set me straight.

He told me God had given him a word for me. He's a super sweet guy, so I got excited. Maybe He was going to tell me I was doing a great job! Maybe He was going to tell me to keep going!

Instead, the sweet college student's expression grew stern, and he said, "God wants you to stop being self-deprecating about our church. Stop calling it weird." Well, um, okay. For the record, I'd never said our church is weird to this guy. In fact, I hadn't said it to anyone who goes to our church. Mostly I just called it weird in my heart.

I blinked and nodded and said, "Okay. Thank you. I will. For sure."

"That's not all," he said. "God also wants you to stop calling your body weird. Stop being self-deprecating about what He has called good."

Um, okay, God. You don't have to get so specific.

A few weeks before this, I'd sat in my counselor's office, opening up to her about some current body image issues, and the interesting thing was that I kept using the word *weird*. I didn't think it was interesting, but she did. She asked if I noticed that I was using the word *weird* quite frequently, and even pointed out what a juvenile word it is. To which I replied that I think a lot of these feelings *are* juvenile for me.

When something doesn't fit in, when something isn't standard, when it's not like everyone else or its surroundings, the way I feel about it is similar to when I was the girl who didn't fit in at the lunch table in middle school. I feel weird.

But often, in the kingdom, things are weird because they're *right*. Because they're obedient. And when it comes to my body, I'd momentarily forgotten that my aim isn't to be a cookie-cutter version of what the world calls good—I'm here to magnify and glorify God, my Father and creator.

Hearing from God is not weird; it's biblical. Don't make the mistake I did by disagreeing with His Word and His way. Let's name it good and live like we believe it.

2. Your capacity is not the variable.

If this book has taught you one thing so far, I pray it's this: what will be accomplished in your life has everything to do with God's capacity and nothing to do with yours. Your ability to hear from God is not even on the table as a question in this equation.

If He wants to communicate with you, He will not wait until you're perfect or even until you're adequate, because He knows that day is not coming anytime soon. He wants your willingness to hear—that's it.

If you feel like you can't hear from God because of some past sin, then by all means repent, but know that He has used and communicated with sinners since the beginning, and He is not shocked by your secrets.

If you feel like He can't talk to you or share His vision for your life because you're not smart enough or godly enough, you are ultimately questioning His power. And we know better than to do that, right? Right?

You are not the variable here. The experiences you will have with God do not depend on your merit or the measure of your worth. And if they did—*if* they did—remember that God measures your worth at the highest possible value: He'd give everything for you. And Jesus? He'd leave the ninety-nine to get to you.

3. There are a million mediums.

If you earnestly ask God to give you a vision for your life, there are a million (maybe a billion?) different ways He could meet that request.

He may give you dreams, He may put thoughts in your head. He may bring a word from another person, He may show you something through a movie or a TV show (remember *Alice in Wonderland* and *Grey's Anatomy*?). He may speak to you through a passage of Scripture. He may prompt you to write a mission statement. He may give you vision through a song or impart perspective through a sermon.

I don't know how the Holy Spirit is going to bring you a picture of what He has for your life. I don't know if He's going to show you the very next step, three of the next steps, a figurative metaphor to keep you going, or a literal description of the future.

I just know that nothing is off limits for Him, and I'm wildly excited to see what happens when you take Him at His Word.

4. His Word is the test.

So what happens when He *does* bring the vision? How do you know if it's Him? For reference, can I tell you just a few real-life ways that real people I know have heard from God about something He had for them in the future?

My mom once got direction for her life ministry from a dream about Shania Twain.

Nick, my husband, heard God call him to plant a church during a drive in the car.

I knew a woman who felt like she was supposed to tithe an extra few dollars because she found it in her car.

My sister felt called to start a business when she was drawing on a napkin during a mission trip.

My friend Hannah perceived God telling her to move during a meditation session.

Once during a run, God told me where our church would be located, and then, it happened.

These are just a few examples of situations that were seemingly out of the blue but which God used to speak to His people.

These are also scenarios in which I was closely involved, and so, as much as possible, I can vouch for their veracity. How? How can I know these things were of God and not just weirdos putting words in God's mouth to do what they wanted to do anyhow?

The Word.

In all these scenarios, if I unpack what each of those people perceived God to be saying or speaking and why, what you'd hear is that all of them line up with God's Word. This means we have to know His Word, or at least be willing to fact-check a little.

If what you think He might be saying is consistent with the Word of God, even if it's spelled out in your kid's SpaghettiOs, you're probably safe.

5. The small stuff matters.

And while we're on the topic of SpaghettiOs, I'd like to make a case for the mundane.

If you ask God for vision for your life, and He gives it in a really simple way—even through ration and reason, through logical steps that make sense—I say praise God.

If you notice you've got a free afternoon, maybe ask to watch your neighbor's kids to bless her.

If your church sends out a massive email asking for more volunteers, that might be for you.

If your coworkers ask what you were doing when you were at Bible study, that could be an invitation to testify.

You made a batch of muffins that are delicious? Make a dozen more and drop them off to a college student or the new mom down the street.

If you think of a cool way to communicate a truth you've just learned in the Word, maybe share it on Facebook.

When you realize you're naturally gifted at putting together flower arrangements, take one to someone who could use some cheering up and maybe slip them an encouraging card, too.

Does it serve others and bring glory to God? Then it doesn't matter how small or mundane it seems. You know what *won't* change the world? Abstaining from the simple, small, life-giving things you were meant to do because you believe they're too simple or too small. That doesn't change the world at all.

We know that sometimes He works in the supernatural, and we know that when He works in the natural, the seen, and the understandable, it's still otherworldly and amazing. Please, please don't discount your interactions with God if the math works and He is actually calling you to the next right step.

6. It's better when it's not all about us.

I'm not the police when it comes to receiving vision from God, so the last thing I want to do is put too many tenets on what He'll say, how He'll say it, or how you should receive it. I don't even want to assign quantitative value to the checks and balances system for sorting out what He seems to be imparting.

But *this* feels like a highly important question to me, one we should ask when we think we've received vision from God:

Is what we believe we're being called to good for anyone else?

I think that God is big enough, personal enough, and good enough to give us visions for our life that have nothing to do with anyone else. I think He has enough vision to go around; He's not going to run out. And I think there may be times when

He shows us something that is *just for us*—we don't have to share it, and it isn't for the consumption of the collective.

But. If *every* goal we've got and every detail of what we are aiming for is *only for our own benefit*, I think that's a good sign we can hit the brakes and ask, *Is this good for anyone else? Does this serve anyone else? Will more people come to know Him, see Him, experience Him when I act in obedience?*

Just a thought that's worth holding and pausing on, amen?

Now, go. Run. Get out of here.

Get with the real Author of it all and see what He wants to say.

You are the girl for the job, and you're the only one who can obediently act on what He is calling you to.

CHAPTER 15

ABUNDANCE HERE AND NOW

JOSEPH WAS THE MOST PATIENT

The story of Joseph in the Bible has always been one of my absolute favorites.

What's interesting to me is this: if I'm in a great season, I can learn a lot from how *blessed* Joseph was, and when I'm on the struggle bus, I learn from his affliction. God dealt with Him abundantly in both, and Joseph praised God through both, so let's dive in together and squeeze as much wisdom from this story as possible.

Abraham, the man God promised would father generations, was the great-grandfather of Joseph. Joseph was the beloved son of Jacob, the first son birthed by Jacob's favorite wife. He didn't just receive favor from God, Joseph also had a beautiful gift from God: a vision that specifically played out in dreams and his ability to interpret them. We'll see how other people's aggravation over Joseph's dreams cost him, but please pay close attention to what they also *purchased* for him. I believe we'll find that his vision paved the way for life-changing patience.

> Joseph had a dream. When he told it to his brothers, they hated him even more. He said, "Listen to this dream I had. We were all out in the field gathering bundles of wheat. All of a sudden my bundle stood straight up and your bundles circled around it and bowed down to mine."
>
> His brothers said, "So! You're going to rule us? You're going to boss us around?" And they hated him more than ever because of his dreams and the way he talked. He had another dream and told this one also to his brothers: "I dreamed another dream—the sun and moon and eleven stars bowed down to me!"
>
> When he told it to his father and brothers, his father reprimanded him: "What's with all this dreaming? Am I and your mother and your brothers all supposed to bow down to you?" Now his brothers were really jealous; but his father brooded over the whole business. (Genesis 37:5–11 MSG)

Joseph's older brothers resented his favored position, so they plotted to kill him—then, when an opportunity presented itself for them to make money, they decided to sell him into slavery instead of murdering him. His father was devastated, but Joseph's story was far from over.

> After Joseph had been taken to Egypt by the Ishmaelites, Potiphar an Egyptian, one of Pharaoh's officials and the manager of his household, bought him from them.

As it turned out, God was with Joseph and things went very well with him. He ended up living in the home of his Egyptian master. His master recognized that God was with him, saw that God was working for good in everything he did. He became very fond of Joseph and made him his personal aide. He put him in charge of all his personal affairs, turning everything over to him. From that moment on, God blessed the home of the Egyptian— all because of Joseph. The blessing of God spread over everything he owned, at home and in the fields, and all Potiphar had to concern himself with was eating three meals a day. (Genesis 39:1–5 MSG)

Okay! We've got a turn in the story. God's favor again! Here's the thing about Joseph and us: everything that seems bad can also be seen as a blessing. If this were a book about seeing the glass half full, we'd camp out here. Instead, let's move on.

Next up, in Genesis 39, Joseph is falsely accused of rape by Potiphar's wife, because he refuses to sleep with her and she gets angry. He is thrown in jail, but God never leaves him. We established earlier that our Father is mighty in the shadows, but let's hear exactly what happened:

But there in jail God was still with Joseph: He reached out in kindness to him; he put him on good terms with the head jailer. The head jailer put Joseph in charge of all the prisoners—he ended up managing the whole operation. The head jailer gave Joseph free rein, never even checked on him, because God was with him; whatever he did God made sure it worked out for the best. (Genesis 39:19–23 MSG)

In Genesis 40, we find Joseph . . . still in jail!

However, he's been put in charge of Pharaoh's cupbearer and Pharaoh's head baker. Pharaoh has gotten very upset with them, for some unknown reason (bad gluten-free cupcakes?) and they've been thrown in jail. Not only that, they're having crazy dreams.

Well, well, well. We know a guy who happens to specialize in dreams, don't we?

Joseph interprets the cupbearer's dream and the baker's dream and tells them that one of them will die and one will be restored to his position (the cupbearer lives; apparently, Pharaoh don't play when it comes to bad muffins), and his interpretation proves correct. Joseph asks the cupbearer to remember him so maybe he can finally get out of jail, but then—the cupbearer forgets.

Every year or so, I study the story of Joseph again to see what God might have for me in it. This year, as I was studying, one verse got me good in the gut:

When two full years had passed, Pharaoh had a dream. (Genesis 41:1)

FULL STOP. Hold up. When two years had passed. When TWO YEARS had passed?!

Two years of waiting. On top of the number of years Joseph had already been waiting? After being sold into slavery, wrongfully accused, and put in jail? Two more years passed?

These were surely complicated days of waiting—full of pain, more downs than ups, and no assurance from any human being that everything was going to be all right. Because we know Joseph was human, we can only assume that those two years were hard and discouraging. I mean, he was in jail. But we also know that because of how he responds when God brings healing and restoration to his life, he could not have been writhing in bitterness and seething with frustration.

When he does finally get out of jail—because Pharaoh needs his gifts—he does not stomp his feet or throw a fit. And I believe we can see at least one reason Joseph was a man of great patience.

Because he was a man of great vision.

Joseph let God show him things, and he believed them. He believed so wholly in a future promised by God that nothing could shake him in his present. That's the power of vision.

Not only did Joseph have God-given prophetic dreams that he could hold on to, but God also gave him the ability to interpret the dreams and visions of others. This took root in his heart, and I'm assuming it led to a great deal of hope welling up inside him.

There are going to be moments of incredible pain, confusion, hurt, and doubt as we obediently answer God's call. There will be shadow moments when we feel as if we're left hanging, questioning whether God—or anyone else, for that matter—remembers us.

And vision is one beautiful tool He places in our hands to help us keep going.

THE ONE WHO KNOWS WHERE YOU'RE GOING

If you've made it this far, I want to give you some insider info.

You know it because you've heard me say it approximately 3,012 times now: you are the girl for the job. YOU.

But since we're in this deep together, I'll be honest with you and tell you I've got a good amount of fear about this power-packed truth and how it can be misconstrued. I'll tell you what I love about it first: I love it because I think almost every woman I know doubts her capacity to live the life to which God has called her. My mama friends feel like they can't do it. The gals in college that I know wonder if they'll ever make it in the real world and question whether they can hack it once they get there. My business friends feel like frauds, and they're sure they're the only ones faking it till they make it. My Christian author friends, present company included, feel inadequate because they know the ugly (beautiful) truth: they're not any closer to God than you are or any more equipped to talk about Him than your super-wise friend who will never get a publishing deal.

My husband, who is a pastor, worries that he's not the right guy for the job. My daughter, who is ten, is already beginning to question her ability to be what the world wants her to be. *Everyone* struggles with this, and that makes me love the message of this book, because I so want to encourage *everyone* right where they're at.

Here's what I don't love about it: the answer isn't within *us*. We are not the heroes. The last thing I want is for anyone to think I'm selling a gospel that says we can do this on our own. To be honest, not only do I know I can't do this on my own, but I don't even know that I can help God get it all done.

Once, when I was really sick, I had to take a shuttle from a conference where I was speaking to the airport, which was two hours away. My flight was pretty early, so the shuttle picked me up around 5 a.m., and I was so violently ill, I could barely hold my head up straight. I texted my husband and shared the location of my iPhone with him, then crawled to the back of the fifteen-passenger van and passed out in a sickly stupor. I was thankful to wake up at the airport two hours later and not at some warehouse where I could have been driven for torturous purposes. I was grateful to get where I was supposed to be going.

This story has a point.

You know how people talk about God being your copilot?

Personally, I'd like to assert that God is not the copilot of my life.

Rather, He's like the very benevolent and all-knowing driver who knows where we're going, how to get there, and why we're headed there in the first place.

Writing, for me, is like sharing the location on my phone. When I'm passed out in the back of the van, I have so little control over the situation, but I will report in on where He takes me on the way, and I will trust that it will be somewhere good.

Having vision matters, not because the pressure is on us to know where we're going, but because it reminds us that God is the one driving. He is the one in control. And He is *so kind* and *so loving* to give us a heads-up about where the van is headed.

He is the hero, we are grateful to be a part of His rescue plan, and having vision reminds us to look to the One who is driving. For answers, for worship, for wisdom and comfort and healing and help.

GOD-CENTERED VISION AFFORDS US ABUNDANCE RIGHT NOW

Lord, You alone are my portion and my cup;
you make my lot secure.

The boundary lines have fallen for me in pleasant
   places;
surely I have a delightful inheritance.
I will praise the Lord, who counsels me;
even at night my heart instructs me.
I keep my eyes always on the Lord.
With him at my right hand, I will not be shaken.
   (Psalm 16:5–8)

Show me a woman who knows where God has called her but who holds progress in high regard, and I'll show you a woman who understands abundance.

Show me a woman who knows that vision affords her patience but has patience to see the vision God has given her come to fruit, and I'll show you a woman who understands abundance.

Show me a gal who does not have time to compare the lives of other women because she is furiously busy thanking God for where He has brought her, and I'll show you a woman who understands abundance.

If the vision leaves you frustrated and feeling fruitless because you're not there yet, you have missed the main characteristic of the mission altogether. Simply put: you are blessed that you get to go on this journey *with* God. He knows that joy and abundance are waiting for you inside of it.

If any part of us believes that our job is to receive vision from God and obediently answer His call on our lives so that we will be happy and blessed and living the dream, then we've got to pause.

Because the ability to respond to Him, to answer His call with our lives, our gifts, our strengths, our weaknesses, and our story *is* the dream. This is the dream. Right now.

Sister-friend, please remember that I'm writing from the shadows and that my ministry life is *not* the world's dream right now. In fact, it's some people's nightmare. We don't have enough money; we don't have enough volunteers. (I'm currently running the kids' ministry, and if you knew me at all, you'd spit out your coffee and say, "Oh! It *really* isn't your dream, is it?") We've been falsely accused; we've been rightly accused. We've come up short, and we've felt wildly disappointed in people who promised us things they just couldn't deliver. It feels like we've been living on manna for months and we'd give just about anything for a bagel. Holler if you hear me, say amen if you're picking up what I'm putting down. This church-planting life might actually do me in.

But then I remember.

I was the least likely to succeed, and I bullied a girl named Molly when I was in middle school. I barely graduated high school, and I was dating a drug dealer when I was in seventh grade. I remember that by nature, I'm a lazy liar who is out for her own good—but then Jesus grabbed my heart when I was fifteen, and everything changed.

Well. Everything *started* changing. He spent thirteen years working on my heart and refining my desires, and He took the least likely person to ever tell anyone about Jesus and placed her in a leadership role at a church.

And then He kept working on her. He gave her friends and confidants and books and the Holy Spirit. And the grace kept coming. She kept messing up and doing it wrong and dragging her heels, and He just had the sun keep on rising, and He made her heart keep growing, and *He keeps showing up.*

So sure. I can sit here in the shadows, frustrated that my

vision has not yet come to fruition, or I can thank the God of the Universe that His grace has grabbed me and placed me in a situation I could never have earned. I can remember that the process is absolutely the place to start praising Him. I can thank God for the blessing and honor to play any role in His house.

I can declare that the boundary lines have fallen in pleasant places for me, and I can experience abundance.

Ask God for vision. Ask Him for more than you could picture or imagine. Ask Him for wisdom and perception and a picture of where you're headed. I believe He'll give it to you, in some shape or form, and I believe it will change the way you walk and run with Him.

But while you're there, ask Him for joy on the way—because vision affords us the ability to believe that abundance is right here and right now. And vision reminds us that we are the girls for the job—not in the future, but today. And that is a gift we don't deserve.

MAKE YOUR MOVE

Abundance comes from obedience.
Let's go!

CHAPTER 16

THE MOST IMPORTANT STEP
Make Your Move

In the one-on-one coaching sessions I do with women, we spend almost all day walking through the first five steps I've just outlined for you. Truthfully, I hate calling them steps. This process is wildly worshipful for me, and the last thing I want to do is make it sound mechanical or emotionless. But for simplicity's sake—yeah, let's call them steps.

It takes us all day to walk through the five steps, and I love watching women come alive. Often, a woman won't really know why she's come to me for coaching when she first walks in—or at least, she can't verbalize it. Then, by the time we get to casting a vision, she's telling me that in five years she wants to have started a ministry for single mothers in her town. She's telling me she wants to pay off her best friend's wedding with profits from her small business. In the span of a few hours, the dreams and aspirations of her heart have been given meaning, purpose, and direction.

So we set aside just a little time at the end of the day for her to make a move. Nothing extravagant or boisterous—I just want to see her take one tiny action step that will help her agree with what she has expressed all day long.

And almost always, this is where the wheels fall off.

If she feels compelled to start a business, I might suggest that she buy a domain name for her website. It's a twelve-dollar investment that makes people feel massively legit but takes just five minutes and very little money. It's not a whole website, but it's the promise of one, the potential of one.

If she feels like God is calling her to write or publish, I might have her send an email or two to a few publishing agents about setting up a meeting, or I may even suggest she buy the domain of the book title she wants to use.

Maybe God has called her to ministry in her hometown, so I'll suggest she email a few friends and put a date on the calendar for a prayer night. That way there is an appointed time when she is on the hook to share what God has put on her heart and she can't get out of it.

Whatever it is, we take a small step together that *agrees* with all the things she's said throughout the day. And with this many years of coaching under my belt, I am now fairly certain I will see her crack a little at this point.

When it's time to buy the domain, she begins to get flustered and can't find her credit card, or she looks at me nervously before she hits send on the email to her friends. The first step is the scariest, but it's also the most important.

I wonder if some of you have known your first step since before you picked up this book. I wonder if you haven't already felt the pulsating desire to take any of the following "steps" for some time now:

Send the email

Draft the text message

Walk over to your neighbor's house

Open the bank account

Call the adoption agency

Download the info guide

Visit the church

Write the first draft

Write down the prayer request

Send the check

Buy the domain

Delete the app

Download the app

Open the Bible

Drop to your knees and start praying

Maybe you need the permission of this chapter and these words to hear: *This is the hardest part for everyone.* It's not just you! It's me, too.

Even those of us who've already started, who may be in the thick of the mission to which God has called us may feel a tug to a new thing, a tug to a new way, a Spirit-driven surge within us compelling us to do what we do with more fervor or in a new direction.

And while we're so simply calling these parts of our process "steps," let me tell you: I take these steps over and over again. I'll text a friend and say, "I need to quit a few things—can I tell you about it?" or I'll write out my fears on a notepad, just so I can answer them with truth. I have to take the first simple step over and over again.

I'd like to present Exhibit B, a real text I sent my husband this morning:

> Will you help me think through something we can do as a family this week that will help us fulfill the Great Commission? Not lead others to do it, but will help US do it? I can brainstorm ideas, too, if you need help. We'll make time for it. I'm just feeling that itch to be the hands and feet of Jesus outside the church.

We talked it over later and landed on something crazy simple and attainable that fits the vision God has given us and our time constraints, but also causes us to stretch a little.

We're buying the teachers at our kids' school some fun treats to enjoy before the PTA meeting this week and taking our kids to serve them.

It's not wild or risky, and we won't win any awards for it. But it's a small step of obedience toward a larger vision we have for our lives, which is this: we want to be so impactful, loving, and kind toward the people who work at our kids' school that if something happened to us, they'd miss us. It's not because we want to be the heroes; it's because we know that the light of Christ shines when the people of God show up. And we love these teachers and want them to know how much Jesus loves them, too.

You are the girl for the job.

So step up to the plate.

Take one tiny step forward.

Take one small step that agrees with the vision, the mission, and the identity that's been imparted to you by the power of the Holy Spirit.

TELL A FRIEND, MAKE IT REAL

What if you want to make a move, but you're not quite there yet?

I've got a safe little bridge you can pass over if you're still unsure, or a victory lap you can take if you've already made the big step.

During those all-day coaching sessions I've been telling you about, women are often hesitant to take the leap or even just dip a toe in the waters of obedience. You know what's often even harder for them than taking the first step? Telling a friend what they're up to.

Why? Because telling a friend makes it real. It means no turning back. It's making a claim that your vision is legitimate, and you are making moves on it. This is scary stuff!

Often, a woman will come for coaching with me, and she'll have flown in from across the country or driven hours to get there, and I'll be massively admiring her bravery to do something so bold. Honestly, I'd be terrified to drive a handful of hours to meet with some woman who wants to help me accomplish my God-given goals.

I imagine I'd ask my friends to pray for me if I was even *thinking* about going. And then I'd send them a website to look over the information, and I'd probably pick a Scripture to ask them to pray over me before going into the coaching session, and I'd take extra time on my bathroom breaks to send them updates.

I am a *groups girl*. I roll deep. I don't do anything alone.

So imagine my surprise when I realize in almost all of my coaching sessions that the beauty sitting before me is not only there bravely alone, but she has also kept it a secret that she's there. If she's married, her husband knows, but it's pretty rare that someone has told their friends or family what they're up to.

And I get it, because so many of us are working through those fears of rejection or people thinking we think we're special, but I often think it's more than that. I think it's that phoning a friend, allowing someone else to bear witness to what we're doing, makes it real—and then we can't take it back.

So I'm going to encourage you right now to kick Satan in the actual teeth and phone a friend. It doesn't have to be a literal phone call. It can be a text, an email, a handwritten letter, or setting up a coffee date. Just reach out in some way that legitimizes the action step you are going to take or have already taken. Bring her in, ask for her help, or at the very least, ask her to pray with you.

Now, let's take it one step further.

Do you need to phone a friend and take on a partner in this endeavor? I've found that, for me, autonomy can often be the enemy of humility. When I'm insistent that I need to do something on my own, it's often because (A) I don't want anyone to see me fail, (B) I don't want anyone else to share the credit, or (C) I believe that if someone else weighs in, corrects, or affects my mission, my progress will be compromised.

Grabbing a friend to partner with you *will* do all of these things. Our pride will be exposed, and someone else might see us falter. We may not be seen as the hero if we're part of a team or a collaborative effort. And there's no doubt about it—we'll be slowed down, and our sole initiative will be hindered and altered when we allow another person to analyze it. But in the name of Jesus, I believe all of these things can be beneficial for the kingdom of God.

I don't presume to think that every act of obedience for the glory of God and the good of others should be a group effort.

But I don't think it's a horrible idea to hold this question in our hearts: Is this something you've asked me to do on my own, or would a partner be a blessing to me and the kingdom?

> It's better to have a partner than go it alone.
> Share the work, share the wealth.
> And if one falls down, the other helps,
> But if there's no one to help, tough!
>
> Two in a bed warm each other.
> Alone, you shiver all night.
>
> By yourself you're unprotected.
> With a friend you can face the worst.
> Can you round up a third?
> A three-stranded rope isn't easily snapped.
> (Ecclesiastes 4:9–12 MSG)

You are the girl for the job, but do not rob your people of the opportunity to experience His call on your life *with* you. Let's also not rob ourselves of the experience of sharing the work and sharing the wealth. Our Father designed us to go together—so let's grab a friend and ask for help.

KEEP A RECORD

Can I implore you to add one more facet to your simple step of obedience?

Keep a record.

I already told you that my favorite Gospel, maybe my favorite book in the New Testament, is the book of Luke. Here's why:

Luke, the author of both the book of Luke and the book of Acts, is barely described in Scripture, but here's what we do know: Colossians 4:14 tells us that he was a doctor by trade. Luke also tells us that he was intentionally writing his book as an account for someone named Theophilus. The name Theophilus means "friend of God" or "lover of God," so there are lots of debates about what that means in regard to the person for whom Luke was writing.

Some theologians think it means he was writing to believers who were yet to come—that he was recording the story of Jesus' life and the early church for the lovers of God who would need to one day hear the story. Some people think he was writing to an actual person named Theophilus, a government official or an influential citizen. There are also theories that Theophilus was Luke's benefactor—his boss, so to speak, who sent him to get eyewitness accounts of Jesus' life and ministry.

So I love that Luke is writing intentionally, but I also love that because of his background as a physician and the nature of his writing, it's commonly agreed upon that his Gospel was a detailed, organized, and fact-checked account. This is not an emotional plea from one person's perspective—it's a record. It's reporting.

When Nick first told me he felt called to plant a church, I was wildly opposed to the idea for a million reasons. But he won my heart when he sat me down and made a passionate plea for me to be his Luke. He told me he wanted me to record all that God was doing and would do. I took that call seriously, and it's been my joy to document our journey—privately, online, and in stories like the ones I've shared in this book.

I'd love to spur you on today toward that same good work: *keep a record.*

Take pictures of your feet the day you make an obedient step. Make a quick journal entry on your darkest day. Write a handwritten letter to a friend telling her the highs and lows of this season.

I do this by taking a video for Instagram Stories every Sunday for our prayer circle. Our service starts at 10:30, but at 9:30 we gather for prayer with any leaders who are present. It's how we intentionally set the temperature before our congregation arrives. So every Sunday, right when prayer begins, I take a quick video of everyone's feet standing in the circle. On the rare occasion that I can't be at church on a Sunday, it will delight me to no end when someone else takes the video and posts it on social media, usually tagging me and telling me they filled my place.

These videos started out as a way for me to mark each week, but I can't tell you how many people have reached out to me to say it's sparked them to want to go back to church or to start similar prayer gatherings in their cities. I created a hashtag, #diariesoftheplanterswife, on Instagram, so I could collect moments and memories, whether good, great, or gruesome. I've begun collecting testimonies—beautiful and bold ones, as well as quietly fruitful ones—asking people to write down their stories so I can have a record of what God is doing in our midst. Each morning, when I spend time with God, I "count the fruit" by writing down just a few ways I've seen His grace expressed in my life in the last twenty-four hours.

As you make a move, as you make the next move, as you eventually plow forward in expectant obedience, *keep a record*. When He brings momentum or asks you to pause, when He does more than you could ask or imagine, *keep a record*.

You'll find that it encourages your heart, that it motivates you to keep moving. On hard days or in dark seasons, it will remind you of the provision you've already experienced. But I also pray, in the name of Jesus, that your individual stories will spur on and inspire the Theophiluses for generations to come.

You are the girl for the job.

It's time to make a move.

CHAPTER 17

A FEW MORE THINGS BEFORE YOU GO

We don't have to look too far to see beautiful, vibrant examples of people who took God at His Word regarding their respective missions, because they're literally everywhere. But I want to go straight to my favorite source for an intentional reason. If we want to see a good example of someone using what they've got for the good of others and the Glory of God, we don't have to look further than Jesus.

I love to watch where He goes and who He talks to; I love to see the weight of His words as they hit the people around Him. Right now, I'm sitting in a coffee shop with a ginormous smile on my face because even though today I'm a little tired, I'm remembering what Jesus did, and it's bringing me an involuntary burst of joy.

If ever we feel burned out on religion or talk of God, please, Holy Spirit, stir us up to remember that Jesus was God in human form, God made flesh. He walked on earth and prayed for us and hung on a cross and loved people with all He had. Help us to remember that He's still alive and interceding on our behalf. Help us to picture His eyes, His hands, and His compassion.

Here's what I know about Jesus: He was on mission. He knew He was the guy for the job.

Of all the people who would ever seek to serve others for the sole purpose of glorifying God, Jesus alone could do it in His own strength, as He was fully God. And yet He submitted Himself to the constraints of humanity so He could be fully present with us and step in as a sacrifice for the sins of the world.

So what does one do when one is completely divine and also living under the constraints of humanity? Jesus worshipped.

When all the people were being baptized, Jesus was baptized too. And as he was praying, heaven was opened and the Holy Spirit descended on him in bodily form like a dove. And a voice came from heaven: "You are my Son, whom I love; with you I am well pleased." (Luke 3:21–22)

Then Jesus looked up and said, "Father, I thank you that you have heard me. I knew that you always hear me, but I said this for the benefit of the people standing here, that they may believe that you sent me." (John 11:41–42)

Very early in the morning, while it was still dark, Jesus got up, left the house and went off to a solitary place, where he prayed. (Mark 1:35)

We see a Jesus in Scripture who prays, goes away to spend time with God, worships and sings hymns with His disciples, talks to God corporately, gets honest with God, gets angry in front of God, cries out to His Father, and takes advantage of His access to God.

May it be the same for us, sisters.

May we take what we need from the throne room of grace as our intercessor offers it.

> Now that we know what we have—Jesus, this great High Priest with ready access to God—let's not let it slip through our fingers. We don't have a priest who is out of touch with our reality. He's been through weakness and testing, experienced it all—all but the sin. So let's walk right up to him and get what he is so ready to give. Take the mercy, accept the help. (Hebrews 4:14–16 MSG)

You can worship on your way. You can talk to your Father as you go. You don't *have* to read the Bible—you *get* to spend time with the Word of Life for wisdom and encouragement. This is your spiritual act of worship, your obedient offering of your gifts and strengths to the world for His glory and their good. But it's also your worship, so don't forget to take what you need on the way.

THE SUN ON YOUR FACE + THE WIND AT YOUR BACK

In the summer of 2017, Nick and I went back to the Pacific Northwest, almost on a pilgrimage, to see what we'd missed when we lived out there. It had been such a rough season in our lives, and we always sensed that we'd missed the best the region had to offer. I was struggling with depression when we lived there, we had no money, and we had three tiny babies. We weren't free to do all the sightseeing.

So we saved our money and our babysitting favors and flew back across the country together for an anniversary trip. In preparation, we made a long list of all the places we'd always wanted to visit. One such place was Deception Pass, this beautiful bridge/hiking area in the northwest part of Washington State.

First, I'm pretty sure Washington State in the summer is what heaven will look like. The air is crisp, cool, and comfortingly warm all at once. Beneath your feet and literally all around you the landscape is a green that looks like it's on fire, as though lit from the inside. There are sparkling blades of grass and branches of emerald all around, rustling in the wind and dancing in the breeze. And Deception Pass itself is a beautiful old bridge connecting two islands, but the heights of the bridge and surrounding mountains combined with the expanse of the sandy beaches on the islands' shores is just too much to take in. It's too beautiful.

Nick and I drove around, trying to open our eyes wide, taking mental pictures with our brains and actual pictures with our cameras as we hiked up what we hoped was the highest peak in the area. And I'm not going to lie, it was a steep one. The incline on the way up was densely lined with trees, so we couldn't actually see anything for a long time but the dirt beneath our feet and the green-on-fire branches deepened by the shadows of the tree cover all around us.

My legs were pretty achy, and my back was kind of a mess from the long plane ride we'd just taken. But we pressed on, sure that what was ahead was worth it.

As we reached the tip-top of the mountain, we both got very quiet, and we emerged out of the forest and into a clearing in silence. Blinking back the brightness, we turned slowly around, letting the sight simmer into memory. The blues of the water seemed otherworldly, and I've already told you about the greens, but I just stood there, seeing the beauty, feeling the sun on my face and the wind blowing comfortingly at my back.

And the Holy Spirit said, *This is what mission is like.*

When you're walking with Me, obeying My commandments for your life, only you can feel the ache of your legs, and only you can sense just how hard it often is to keep going. People can promise you there's a clearing up ahead, but the shadows will be so deep and thick, it will be hard to take anyone else's word for it.

But when you step into the sun? When you finally reach the place where your perspective collides with horizon and you see the thing you've been walking toward, no one will be able to take away how it feels to have the sun on your face and the wind at your back.

It might seem crazy, but I knew God was using this hike to show me that running on mission is better for my life. It's not what He needs *from* me; it's what He wants *for* me. He wants me to keep going so I can have the perspective and feel the warmth of His presence.

Moreover, I feel like He brought that season of our lives in the PNW full circle for me. We never missed out on seeing the best parts of the PNW when we lived there. Sure, I spent a lot of time changing diapers in a basement apartment. I spent many hours rocking babies and comforting women in coffee shops. Shoot—I spent a lot of time being comforted myself in coffee shops! We shed a lot of tears and prayed a lot of prayers, but the sun was on our faces and the wind was at our backs. We were changing the world with what we had; we were showing up and letting the light shine in and through our darkness.

When you go—when you take these steps of obedience to use what you've got for His glory right where He's put you—will you picture yourself with the sun on your face and the wind at your back? Even when you feel like you're in the absolute depths of the shadows and even when it feels like you've completely been left behind or messed the whole thing up—will you remember with me that this is what we *get* to do? This is His best for us, His gift to us, this invitation to a life of adventurous and abundant mission.

SPREAD THE WORD

As you're going, as you're applying these steps and processes to your own wild and wonderful life of mission—will you spread the word? Will you tell your sister, your mom, your friend, and the girl at your office who might not be your cup of tea, will you tell *them* that they are *also* the girls for the job God has given them?

Will you tell your friend who seems to have it all together that *she* is the girl for the job? Because she's probably terrified to let her walls down; she's probably terrified to show you that she feels inadequate. Will you remember that you lose nothing by encouraging her, and that there is enough of God's favor, grace, and goodness to go around?

Will you tell the messy gals in your community that *they're* the right ones for the job? Will you take a break from wishing they could pull it together and instead just believe that God's grace is working in and through them? What would it look like to celebrate them right where they're at, to be the one pulling in closer when everyone else is pulling away? How might it change their lives to have someone on their team looking for the fruit and believing in brighter days?

The single mom you know.

The college gal finding her way.

The young mother at the playground.

The woman struggling with her newly empty nest.

The friend battling infertility.

The girl who is always heading up the committees and doesn't seem to need a friend.

Your friend whose husband is sick.

Your sister.

Your single friend who is praying for a husband.

The teen girl who babysits for you.

The barista who always knows your name.

Your new employee.

Your boss.

Your daughter.

The next-door neighbor.

The slightly-too-friendly checkout lady you wish you could avoid.

The homeless woman who lives on the corner.

The lady with the ginormous house down the street.

What if you believed in the power of God at work in all their lives, and what if you took this message of His capacity straight to their hearts? Maybe they've never questioned their ability, purpose, or worth, but I'm willing to bet they're just like you. I'm willing to bet with all I've got that it would change their lives to believe that *you* think they are the girls for the job.

What's more: I'm willing to bet it would change the face of eternity if they believed *God* thought they were the girl for the job.

As you're going, tell them. As a side benefit, you might find that as they begin to believe this wild idea that God's capacity is all they need, they'll preach it back to you when you need it most.

CHAPTER 18

YOU'RE DOING IT RIGHT

WITH MY EYES CLOSED

I have this incredible friend, Alisa, who has a gospel-centered fitness ministry called Revelation Wellness. She leads classes and trains leaders all over the country in this ferocious combination of worship and wellness, and I've gotten to exercise with her a handful of times. Every single time has been life-changing, every single time I've cried tears of joy and epiphany, and every single time I've noticed that she has a signature move.

See, Alisa loves to lead women in wellness no matter their shape, size, or fitness level. She wants them to be safe and do things wisely, but she also knows that most of us can do harder things than we think we can if we're willing to try. Alisa knows that most of us are limited by fear. We're scared to do it wrong, and we're scared to be seen doing it wrong, so there is a huge potential blockade between women and worshipful exercise.

Hence, her signature move. If Alisa is leading women in any kind of nonstandard workout move, or any kind of exercise that might make them feel self-conscious or like they look silly, she yells, "YOU'RE DOING IT RIGHT!" over and over again, at the top of her lungs. She's a tiny little human (I should know because I've picked her up. I couldn't help myself—I had to see if I could because she's so cute and compact), but her great, big, bellowing voice screams over and over again: "YOU'RE DOING IT RIGHT!" I've heard her team even got her a megaphone, and I'm sure that only aids in her boisterous encouragement.

Here's what you'd have to be closely paying attention to catch, though. Sometimes when she's yelling "YOU'RE DOING IT RIGHT!" *she closes her eyes.* I've seen her walk slowly through rows of women and gently shut her lids. I've noticed that occasionally, as she stands on the stage, her little peepers will be tightly sealed, and still she'll be screaming, "YOU'RE DOING IT RIGHT!"

I think this is part of her strategy. It's intentional that she doesn't physically *see* women when she affirms their ability to execute the prescribed exercise, because she is not affirming whether or not they're doing the move well. She's not judging them, and she's not assessing their performance—*she is acknowledging their obedience.* More than that, she's acknowledging their *attempt.* Maybe it's even deeper than that—she's affirming their presence, their commitment to being there.

When her eyes are closed, and she says, "YOU'RE DOING IT RIGHT!" the women could be sitting down drinking water. They could be crying on the floor. They could be in downward-facing dog. They could be looking like a crazy person. Or they could be the spitting image of Jane Fonda doing the exercise so well, they're about to steal her job.

It doesn't matter. Alisa is just acknowledging that they're

doing it right because they're there, because they've shown up, because they haven't left.

And that's the picture I've had in my head all along as I've been writing this book.

I don't know your life, and I don't know your relationship with Jesus. I don't know if it's just getting started or if you've been walking with Him longer than I've been alive. You could be paid to talk about God, or you may have never stepped foot inside a church. Some of you, I'm willing to bet, have tried to do good for His glory and seen massive failure. Some of you have not yet tasted defeat, loss, or even really perceived that you need the gospel. There will be women who read this book who have championed other women well, and there will be women who read this book who are the bullies of their communities. Some of you know what you're gifted at, called to, and created for, and others of you feel lost and left behind.

It doesn't matter. I can close my eyes and scream, "YOU ARE DOING IT RIGHT!" I can affirm that *you are the girl for the job* because I am absolutely sure that God has placed you right where you're at, with all that you have, on purpose. I am willing to bet my life and everything that I own that His capacity is more than enough for all that you need. With every breath I take, I get less sure of the world around me and more sure of Him. I am sure He is good. I am sure He is loving. I am sure He is on the move in your life.

Sometimes saying the very stark alternative helps me assert what I mean, so let me put it this way: I can say with my eyes closed and with no actual knowledge of your life that you are the girl for the job, because the opposite of that is so wildly untrue. The opposite would be to say that you're unusable, that you've somehow slipped through His hands and landed in a place where His love can no longer work though you. The opposite of telling you that you're the girl for the job would be to say that there is someone who can be you, live your story, and be loved by God for you, and I don't believe that for even one second.

You are the girl for the job.

Right where you're at.

This I know to be absolutely true.

HIS EYES ARE OPEN

Our Father's eyes are wide open. He sees you for who you are, for where you've been. He is attentive to your past, present, and future in ways you could never imagine. He sees the broad strokes, the themes of life, the details no one else could ever catch. His eyes were open for the private victories and the loneliest moments of defeat. God did not look away when your sin separated you from the Father. Rather, at just the right time, Jesus took a step forward on your behalf. He sees your motivations and your moping, your character and your comparison. He is fully aware of your ability and your capacity, and He has *chosen* you.

> Therefore, if anyone is in Christ, the new creation has come: The old has gone, the new is here! All this is from God, who reconciled us to himself through Christ and gave us the ministry of reconciliation: that God was reconciling the world to himself in Christ, not counting

people's sins against them. And he has committed to us the message of reconciliation. We are therefore Christ's ambassadors, as though God were making his appeal through us. (2 Corinthians 5:17–20)

God wants you as His ambassador, His representative, His friend, and His coworker. And not because He needs you or wants to keep you busy. He wants you running on mission for His kingdom because He knows it's the most thrilling life you'll ever be able to sign up for. It's not because the Father thinks that mission will make you good, but because He knows it's *for* your good. He wants your obedience so that you can experience abundance.

But you are a chosen people, a royal priesthood, a holy nation, God's special possession, that you may declare the praises of him who called you out of darkness into his wonderful light. Once you were not a people, but now you are the people of God; once you had not received mercy, but now you have received mercy. (1 Peter 2:9–10)

His eyes are not closed. He wouldn't take them off you for a second. This was an intentional and perfect choosing, at exactly the right time.

We've got our hands full continually thanking God for you, our good friends—so loved by God! God picked you out as his from the very start. Think of it: included in God's original plan of salvation by the bond of faith in the living truth. This is the life of the Spirit he invited you to through the Message we delivered, in which you get in on the glory of our Master, Jesus Christ. (2 Thessalonians 2:13–14 MSG)

I may not know you, but I'm still telling you you're the girl for the job.

Because He's said it first.

God does know you. He does see you. He loves you more than you could imagine.

And He's placed you where you're at, with what you've got, on purpose, for the good of others and the fulfillment of His glory.

You're the girl for the job. He said so.

If you believe Him, believe in His character and power, and take Him at His Word—it will change the world.

ACKNOWLEDGMENTS

Nick: I feel so uniquely privileged to have a husband who preaches the gospel to me through his words and his actions every day. I am so freed up to encourage others because you continually point me to His truth, His love, and His grace. Also, your early morning Scrabble messages were the fire that fueled this book.

Anna: You are the girl for the job. Thank God you were and are! I'm so grateful for what we've gotten to build together, and I can't wait to keep going, you poetic and noble land mermaid. You opalescent tree shark. I love you, and I couldn't do this without you (or your feet).

Hannah W: Thank you for living with me through the summer of 2018 and living out these words with me. Thanks for always holding tight to His promises for us. I'm so grateful God wrote our stories together, to dream and to work and to love and to learn. Your strength and softness have changed my life.

Mom: There are so many things you've purchased for us in the spiritual and the physical with your obedience and your desire for abundance. This message and the belief in it feels like a part of that parcel. I'm so grateful for you!

Jenni, Stephanie, Alicia, and Harmony: You are the real MVPs. Thank you for handling this book with care and compassion always. Thank you for leading me, guiding me, and always bringing the best gifts to the table.

Meredith L: God used your wisdom and care to turn one of the most bitter seasons in my life into one with some pretty sweet fruit. Thank you.

Kristen Ezsol, Lauren Pavao, Britt Corner, Hannah Arnold, Helen Brooks, Sarah Lacour, Chalice Howard, Caroline Hopper, Annie Downs, Rach Kincaid, Connie Wood, Gabby Lane, and Kennesha Poe-Buycks: Thank you for being the women I get to know and be known by, thank you for being my co-laborers and friends.

Connolly Kiddos: We did it again! Thanks for caring that I write books and getting excited about them. Thanks for putting up with a pretty sleepy mom during the summer of 2018. Cannon, thanks for cuddling with me when I'd write. Glo, thanks for being the woman I most want to be. Benja, your wit keeps me on my toes and keeps me trying to be funny. Elias, watching you fall in love with Jesus has been an inspiration.

New Video Study for Your Church or Small Group

If you've enjoyed this book, now you can go deeper with the companion video Bible study!

In this 6-session study, Jess Connolly helps you apply the principles in *You Are the Girl for the Job* to your life. The study guide includes video notes, group discussion questions, and personal study and reflection materials for in-between sessions.

Study Guide
9780310094197

DVD
9780310094234

Available now at your favorite bookstore,
or streaming video on StudyGateway.com.

Also Available from Jess Connolly

Dance, Stand, Run is an invitation to the daughters of God to step into the movements of abundant life: dancing in grace, standing firm in holiness, and running on mission. Through story and study, Jess casts a fresh vision for how to live into your identity as a holy daughter of God, how to break free of cheap grace and empty rule-keeping, and finally, how to live out your holy influence with confidence before a watching world. Spoiler alert: it's a beautiful thing.

For anyone longing to take their place in what God is doing in the world, *Dance, Stand, Run* will rally your strength, refresh your purpose, and energize your faith in a God who calls us to be like Him.

Book	Study Guide	DVD
9780310345640	9780310090212	9780310090236

Available now at your favorite bookstore,
or streaming video on StudyGateway.com.